THE GENIUS OF NIJINSKY

beaming across time

AF605357

JILL RIVERS

The Genius of Nijinsky
Copyright © Jill Rivers 2025

The Author has asserted their rights under the Copyright Act 1968 (the Act) to be identified as the author of this work.

All rights reserved. No part of this publication may be reproduced, stored in a retrieval system, or transmitted in any form or by any means, electronic, mechanical, photocopying, recording or otherwise, without the prior written permission of the author. Any person who does any unauthorised act in relation to this publication may be liable to criminal prosecution and civil claims for damages.

The Australian Copyright Act 1968 (the Act) allows a maximum of one chapter or ten per cent of this book, whichever is the greater, to be photocopied for educational purposes by an educational institution holding a statutory education licence provided that the educational institution (or body that administers it) has given a remuneration notice to the Copyright Agency (Australia) under the Act.

Front cover drawing by Vaslav Nijinsky, presented to Paul Cox by the Nijinsky family, courtesy Kyra Cox.
Image of Vaslav Nijinsky in Petrouchka

ISBN: 978-1-923289-78-9 (Paperback)

A catalogue record for this book is available from the National Library of Australia

Published by Art-full Living.
Publishing services and printing in Australia by Clark & Mackay

CONTENTS

DEDICATION

To the memories of Paul Cox, who inspired me on the path, and Tamara Nijinsky, who told me to bless all corners of the room to know what to write.

PROLOGUE

I was sitting at a street café in Melbourne, Australia, in 2000 when I was approached by Alida Chase, a former dancer I knew, who told me she was working as a dance consultant on a film being made by filmmaker Paul Cox on Vaslav Nijinsky, the Russian dancer. I had no idea that Cox was interested in dance, let alone that he had been obsessed with Nijinsky for over thirty years.

I was fascinated by both the obsession and the mystique. Nijinsky is a legendary name in the world of dance, which I had recently inhabited for eleven years working with a major dance company, but I had fused his personality with that of Rudolf Nureyev – the male dance icon of more recent times.

My excuse was that my background was not in dance and that there were obvious similarities between them: both were brilliant ballet dancers who had revitalised the role of the male dancer in the 20th century, emigres from their Mother Russia, Nureyev as a defector.

I was intrigued and immediately immersed myself in a book that happened to be on my shelves at home – Nijinsky's biography, written by his wife, Romola.

Nijinsky's wife? That was an immediate confusion. I thought he was the lover of Diaghilev, the great impresario. I searched the local library for further information and eagerly devoured the most recent book available – Peter Ostwald's book *Vaslav Nijinsky: A Leap Into Madness*. It was published in 1992, as opposed to Romola's earlier work of 1933. Although Ostwald's book focuses on Nijinsky's medical condition, there were contradictions galore – were they writing about the same person?

I started randomly asking dancers what they knew of Nijinsky: what did he mean to them? Most of their faces lit up with a look of reverence at his name and some told me of how they had slept with a photo of Nijinsky beside their bed as young aspiring artists. They talked of idolising him as an icon and of his legendary leap, yet few knew any of his details – not even the ballet master of a major company.

Judging by their reactions, and others outside the world of dance, there was a need for Nijinsky's story to be retold. Irrespective of his vital role in the history of dance, his personal story was unfolding as a rich, ripping yarn.

Like Cox, I was hooked – on the hunt to discover the story surrounding this controversial figure.

Cox's connection began in the 1970s when he was in London for a film festival. He heard Nijinsky's diary read by actor Paul Schofield on BBC radio and was "knocked out by Nijinsky's wonderful words – 'You will understand me if you see me dance'," and the fact that Nijinsky communicated through dance – that, for him, it was a primary language. Cox rushed out to buy a copy of the book and was instantly smitten, seduced by Nijinsky's insights into truth, love and beauty. From then, his quest was how to portray that spirit in film.

In 1987, while he was pondering this, Cox made the film *Vincent* – about another extraordinary artist misunderstood by many. In *Vincent*, Cox created a new genre of drama/documentary as he tried to get inside the mind of Van Gogh. I was impressed by his commitment, bordering on obsession.

Nijinsky's diaries reveal how he deplored artificiality and violence. Fascinated by his individuality and genius, Cox identified with Nijinsky's humanitarian qualities and absorbed many of his philosophies. He even named his own daughter after Nijinsky's daughter, Kyra.

A few years later, Cox received an angry letter from Nijinsky's second daughter, Tamara. From her home in Phoenix, Arizona, she had heard him talking of his quest during an interview for a film festival on New York radio. What right did he have to be exploiting her father's name, she demanded; what was his intention? In return, she received a courteous letter from Cox and a copy of his film script. He subsequently flew over to meet the family in Phoenix – Tamara, her daughter Kinga, Kinga's husband John Gaspers and their son – Tamara's grandson – Mark. He came away with their blessings and the rights to the recently (1999) re-published unexpurgated version of *The Diary of Vaslav Nijinsky,* edited by renowned dance critic Joan Acocella in collaboration with Tamara. The original diary, published in 1936 during Nijinsky's lifetime, had been heavily edited by Romola, with toned-down language and numerous omissions.

Cox left Phoenix thinking he was on the way to realising his dream. He decided he would best depict the person of Nijinsky by using his own words, as he had with *Vincent.* He would create a film version of the dancer's diary. "Nobody listened to Nijinsky when he was alive," Cox said, "so I have let him speak."

Cox paid tribute to Nijinsky's poetry by weaving an abstract series of images – a journey through Nijinsky's mind. There was no star in the film, as Cox's concept was to portray the kaleidoscope of characters Nijinsky created in life and on stage and carried in his head.

Tamara, then in her eighties, and her daughter, Kinga Nijinsky Gaspers, endorsed his concept and became his enthusiastic collaborators, advising on the script and imagery.

As soon as he heard of my interest, Cox generously shared his passion and the footage of his film-in-progress and piled me high with further reading. Before I knew it, I too was on a plane to Phoenix, Arizona, courtesy of Cox and Tamara Nijinsky, who had invited me to stay.

My timing was fortuitous: Kinga Nijinsky Gaspers was about to perform in a play based on the life of Romola – *Madame Nijinsky.*

The first stop for me was the Jerome Robbins Dance Division of the New York Public Library. The further I delved, the more I became consumed with the question marks surrounding Nijinsky. Renowned as one the most spectacular dancers the world has ever known, Nijinsky was the first real superstar of the ballet and of the glittering Diaghilev era, the icon of dancers and choreographers, and a role model for all male dancers since his time. Over the years, Nijinsky has been the subject of countless books, biographies and memoirs. His legend lingers and continues to inspire plays, films, literature and ballet, yet much of his life is unclear. Nothing I absorbed gave me an accurate picture of Nijinsky the person.

There have been other male stars since Nijinsky first dazzled the students and teachers of the Imperial Ballet School in St Petersburg in the early 1900s – dancers such as Rudolf Nureyev and Mikhail Baryshnikov. It is now seventy-five years since Nijinsky's death, and the details of his story are not generally known, so why is there so much continuing interest in Nijinsky? Why is it a name that does not die? And why are there still so many unanswered questions?

By then, I was on a quest to find out. It was an enigma that in the year 2000 – the fiftieth anniversary of his death and the year of my visit to Tamara – two plays were produced on Nijinsky – Kinga's in Phoenix, Arizona, and another in Tokyo, Japan – and two films, a major exhibition was mounted by the Dansmuseet in Stockholm and Musee d'Orsay in Paris, and a Nijinsky ballet festival was presented by the Hamburg Ballet in Germany. In that year John Neumeier created the ballet *Nijinsky* for the Hamburg Ballet, which he then staged with the Australian Ballet in 2016 and 2025. Almost every year, a choreographer somewhere in the world produces a new work based on Nijinsky's original concept for *The Rite of Spring.* In 2000, the Australian Ballet and Bangarra Dance Theatre collaborated on producing their own version, *Rites.*

Gradually, a vague outline of the person of Nijinsky began to emerge from the contrasting accounts I had absorbed in my search; from Romola's alternating information, sanitising and omissions; Russian ballet writer Vera Krasovskaya's fascinatingly flowery prose and fantasies; platitudes and gushing reviews; academic studies and analyses; assumptions and jealousies; photographs; articles; talks; and opinions.

When you are on the hunt, I discovered, you often find clues in unlikely places. I found them in almost everything I read: the biographies of Isadora Duncan, Janet Frame and Marcel Proust, as well as the obvious sources. Like the art form of ballet itself, the story of Nijinsky becomes accessible upon exposure. Each time I thought I had exhausted every major record of the time, more became available: the ballet master Grigoriev's account, that of Imperial Ballet star Mathilde Kschessinska, and Diaghilev's close friend and major patron Misia Sert – although not reliable as primary sources – all offered insights that proved invaluable. I could have gone on happily unearthing clues to Nijinsky for another ten years, but my motivation was to relate his story without bias for today's world. That, I discovered, was the challenge. My encounters with the family revealed a legacy almost as complicated and contradictory as his life. I hit barriers that caused me to set the story aside. But it was there to stay. Whether or not it is the "right time," I owe it to the memory of the man I have attempted to understand to remind dancers of his place in their history. Twenty-five years later, I am resuming the story of my quest for Nijinsky's story by telling it as it unravelled – not a biography, but the passing on of the facts as I found them and my experiences in retracing them. Tamara told me to read *The Diary of Vaslav Nijinsky* and I would know what to write. I cannot quote many of his insightful words, and I urge you to read the book yourself. This is the story of how I discovered Nijinsky's genius and began to understand Nijinsky the person.

PHOENIX

My research in the New York Public Library and through other avenues revealed a record of the grandeur of the Nijinsky and

Diaghilev period that was overwhelming. His wife Romola's aristocratic Hungarian family background was impressive and overwhelming. But although there was much information on their eldest daughter, Kyra, there was little about my hostess and guardian of the Nijinsky heritage, the second daughter Tamara.

Her lineage was impressive – daughter of the great Nijinsky, granddaughter of the renowned Hungarian actress Emília Márkus (considered in Hungary with the same respect as Sarah Bernhardt), who had brought her up in Budapest. Added to that, every Hungarian I knew had a dominating personality. I was excited and sick on the flight with apprehension.

I arrived in Phoenix to an amazing sunset, passing over cacti to touch down in this fast-developing city on the edge of the desert. Waiting at the gate as I disembark are two women with a large plaque: *Cox film. Welcome, Jill!* The senior of the two, a small, unassuming-looking American, presents me with a bouquet of flowers.

I am driven to Kinga's home in the suburbs for a three-woman meal they have kindly prepared to meet my vegetarian needs. It is a potato-and-egg Hungarian dish in sour cream that delights Tamara, as it reminds her of her childhood with her grandmother in Budapest. They are warmly hospitable and put me at ease, offering me drinks although not drinkers themselves. They, disarmingly, appear to be a normal American family, with Tamara's proud talk of grandson Mark doing well at college, and no sign at all of being the angry daughter – nor any obvious Hungarian accent.

However, there is a touch of the surreal in that we are eating our meal sitting at the legendary star's wife Romola's dining table, on Romola's chairs, with Romola's cutlery, from her blue and white china plates. The plates are the same as mine in Australia – surely an omen?

After we have eaten, Kinga shows me around her spacious home, which combines modern-day living with much memorabilia. It is largely a shrine to her grandmother – Nijinsky's wife, Romola – as much as Nijinsky.

They tell me that this is the right time for making the film – to "correct" the "commercial" film *Nijinsky* directed by Herbert

Ross in 1980. It featured a star-studded cast of George de la Peña as Nijinsky, Alan Bates as Diaghilev, Leslie Browne as Romola, Jeremy Irons as Fokine, Anton Dolin as Cecchetti and Carla Fracci as Tamara Karsavina.

But to the Nijinsky women, the film was a gross misinterpretation of facts – a big disappointment to them as the culmination of a long-term desire of Romola's to make a film of Nijinsky's life. She had spent years negotiating with Hollywood and a raft of producers, championing first Rudolf Nureyev and then Mikhail Baryshnikov to play Nijinsky. It was the source of great frustration and a litany of aborted attempts. Her spirit is guiding this film of Paul's, Tamara tells me.

After dinner, Kinga drives us to Tamara's modest two-bedroom unit across town. After she leaves, Tamara takes me through the "house rules", which are mostly where the light switches are. Lastly, she tells me to bless all corners of the room before I go to sleep and I will have beautiful dreams. I feel welcome in this warm household. There is such a strong sense of family and belonging.

I am sleeping on a fold-out bed in Tamara's study – also a shrine to her father, with a photo of him as a 17-year-old dominating the room, or so it seems. Surely, I will find the true Nijinsky here. Tamara tells me to re-read his diary and then pray for guidance.

The next morning, as I cautiously leave the house for my daily run, trying not to disturb Tamara, I am overwhelmed by the unreality of the situation. Far from the land of his birth and Europe, where he became known to the Western World, is the headquarters of the Nijinsky Foundation – here in Phoenix, Arizona. Russia, Budapest, Phoenix. It is a massive test of belief to connect this scenario to the Polish/Russian dancer Nijinsky.

At 8 am, the dry heat is stifling. Running beside the canal, I come across few people – a man with a dog, a solitary cyclist. It is already too hot to be out. I make a mental note to run earlier the following day or stay at home. As I arrive back, I hear a call from outside that I can't locate. Tamara is swimming in the pool, a small bathing-capped figure.

We retreat from the desert heat for breakfast and spend the day chatting and examining the Nijinsky exhibits around the room. I am fascinated by his drawings. There are various photos, paintings and a lifetime's worth of icons of the revered, so-called God of the Dance. The man was clearly multi-gifted in the arts.

Tamara is so charming and easy to talk to, intelligent and articulate that I am just able to curb my impatience to begin serious discussions. We are to wait until Kinga has given her performance tonight.

Replete in her grandmother's lipstick – the shade of Helena Rubenstein she always wore – Kinga is wearing Romola's silk pyjamas on the set in the suburb of Scottsdale, surrounded by her grandmother's black Oriental furniture. She delivers a convincing performance of the strong-willed Romola. Now I can see her as her grandmother in my heart.

The next morning, Tamara and I are at last sitting with my tape recorder poised. We talk for three and a half hours, mostly about her elder sister Kyra.

Tamara must have felt a special connection to her father, as he had named her after his long-time dance partner Tamara Karsavina. Although her first memories of him are sitting on his knee, most of her life was spent apart from him. She says that first met Vaslav Nijinsky, the great dancer, through working on the translation of Nijinsky's diary – first published in France. It was a humbling experience to read her father's words as he wrote them. Her goal – her wish and desire – was for people to know him as a human being, that he was a human being who was not in this world.

It was for this reason that she wrote the story of the romance between the young "Hungarian girl and Polish boy"
—*Nijinsky and Romola.*

BACKGROUND

Before I could understand the impact of Nijinsky in Europe in the early 1900s and his pivotal role in the development of dance, I needed to explore the state of dance in Russia at the time and its relationship with the people.

Dance was implanted early in the Russian soul: the Russian mastery of dance and music reaches right back to the ancient community ritual of the circular chain dance – found in the folklore of many nations – which the early Russians performed to slow languid songs on festive occasions.

Professional dance also existed from ancient times, mostly in the form of troupes of entertainers – both men and women – known as *skomorokhi,* famed for virtuoso jumps and acrobatic capers – the forerunners of circus acrobats. There were also female dancers known as *pliassovitsa* and male dancers called *pliassun.* There is a reference from the 16th century to Ivan the Terrible's mother arriving at a court wedding preceded by an entourage of *pliassitsi.*

Over the years, professional dance seesawed in status from low to high entertainment. The tsars were mostly responsible for the acceptance of dance by society and its development as an art form, particularly Peter the Great, whom we know to have been a staunch advocate of Western culture. They introduced the Western form of ballet and sponsored the concept of blending it with the existing form of Russian dance.

It started with the first tsar of the ill-fated Romanov dynasty, Mikhail, who laid the foundations for the Imperial Theatre of later times by setting up an amusement room in his palace. His son Alexei presented the first ballet performance on the Russian stage, *Orpheus and Eurydice*, in the village of Preobrazhenskoye – the summer seat of the tsars, near Moscow – on 8 February 1673. He also founded a court drama theatre and arranged for underprivileged children to have dance training.

Alexei's death in 1676 brought court theatre to an end until early in the 18th century when Peter the Great established a Theatre Room at the Kremlin. It was compulsory for nobles to attend the tsar's assemblies and the Theatre Room radically altered the Russian attitude toward dance. Peter also introduced Western European ballroom dancing at his assemblies and encouraged French and Italian dancers and teachers to set up schools in the country.

The Theatre Room operated until the capital moved to Peter's new Western city of St Petersburg.

In the meantime, the new dance schools were gaining pupils and growing in popularity. On 29 January 1736, a teacher by the name of Jean-Baptiste Landé capped the success of the new vogue by training a hundred pupils of the Corps de Cadets (a military school for young noblemen) to perform the finale of the opera *La forza dell'amore e dell'odio* in a grand dance spectacle at Empress Anna Ioanovna's court. It created such a desire for dance that Landé was able to initiate a three-year professional training course for court dancers, which established ballet as professional theatre. It was later developed into the (prestigious) Imperial School and Theatre.

In 1756, twenty years later, another tsar – Catherine II (the Great) – decreed that the Imperial Theatres be run by the state and, ten years after that, she founded the Directorate of the Imperial Theatres.

Much the same pattern emerged in Moscow, with the great Bolshoi School and Ballet growing out of a dance wing attached to an orphanage. In 1773, Italian dance teacher Filippo Beccari was engaged to train the orphans as professional dancers to entertain the nobility. Moscow rapidly grew into a theatre-conscious city, spawning a succession of venues, including the Znamensky

Theatre (run by Englishman Michael Maddox, who also owned the attached school), the forerunner of the Bolshoi Ballet, where ballets were shown regularly from 1776.

In the same way as the elite build home theatres today, wealthy landowners took up the trend by establishing their own theatres. They selected dancers from their servants or local orphans for these serf theatres on their estates.

The serfs were professionally trained – often by foreign dancing masters – in both the Western European classical ballet *danse d'ecole* and their traditional Russian folk dance.

The serf dancers were beholden to their masters and forced at whim to work in the fields as well as on stage. They were also bidden to participate in orgies on stage "au naturale." As the public theatres gradually gained respect, the fashion for serf theatres began to dwindle and the landowners began to sell their best performers to the government.

After the collapse of one of the major theatre groups – Maddox's enterprise – the Imperial Theatres of Moscow were established in 1806. The last group of thirty-six serf dancers and musicians were bought from the Stolypin estate. In 1861, the serfs were liberated. By that time, all the private groups had disappeared and most of the skilled dancers had been bought by the Imperial Schools.

The present Bolshoi Theatre in Moscow was rebuilt in 1856 by Alberto Cavos – the architect of the two major ballet theatres in Russia today. Cavos was the grandfather of Alexandre Benois, great-uncle of actor/entrepreneur Peter Ustinov and friend and colleague of Sergei Diaghilev, who was to play a major role early in the following century in another major ballet development – the Ballets Russes – and in the life of Vaslav Nijinsky.

Cavos rebuilt the St Petersburg Bolshoi (which was rebuilt in 1896 by the Russian Musical Society and now houses the Conservatory). In 1860, he built the Mariinsky Theatre – the home of the Kirov Ballet, where performances have continued since 1889. I was lucky enough to sense its magic – and sit in the tsar's box – when the Australian Ballet performed on its stage in 1988 on its bicentennial tour of the Soviet Union. The champagne and caviar were replaced by soft drinks and doughnuts during that dour regime, but the mystique and history remained tangible.

By the beginning of the 19th century, Russian ballet was strong and professional, the Imperial Theatres were well established, the school was well organised and the art form had become widely appreciated.

The school had been reformed by the teaching system of another French man, dancer/choreographer Charles Louis Didelot, who introduced the newly developed style of "Romantic" ballet to Russia. A major author and critic of Romantic ballet, Theophile Gautier, noted on his visit in 1858 that ballet was very much more developed in Russia than in France and that "in Petersburg it is not easy to win applause for a *pas*".

Didelot brought the first production of *La fille mal gardée* to Russia in 1827. It was created by his teacher Dauberval and is one of the oldest ballets remaining in the classical ballet repertoire. Didelot also created *Flore et Zephire* for Marie Taglioni's debut at the Paris Opera in 1830; and brought her performance of the Scottish-themed La Sylphide – the first of the "Romantic" ballets – to St Petersburg three years after its 1832 premiere in Paris. A second version choreographed by August Bournonville in 1836 is the only surviving version and the one familiar to modern audiences.

That 1830s and 1840s golden age of Romantic ballet is remembered as the era of the three great ballerinas: Marie Taglioni; Fanny Elssler, in *The Devil on Two Sticks*; and Carlotta Grisi, the first Giselle. They played a major part in the development of the Russian art form. They created their legendary roles in the Romantic fantasies focused on the ballerina that are still central to the classical repertoire today and familiar to audiences worldwide. They often delve into the supernatural, with the *corps de ballet* invariably Wilis, Sylphs (jilted brides and princesses) or other ghosts returning from beyond the grave to tempt or taunt human suitors.

In the second half of the 19th century, Russian ballet was given further impetus by the arrival in St Petersburg in 1847 of Frenchman Marius Petipa – a name we know today as the creator of the most enduring ballets that are still regularly performed. He came from a family of dancers and had been taught by the most respected French dancer and teacher of the time, Auguste Vestris, the first "God of the Dance". Petipa was an established performer and choreographer and had partnered Grisi in *Giselle*.

The work he accomplished in Russia made his name one of the most revered in the history of ballet and one we all recognise. He became chief choreographer and ballet master of the Imperial School and Theatre and dominated ballet in Russia for over forty years.

Petipa reshaped ballet – enlarging the ballet language and its means of expression and achieving a high new standard of artistry. He created a huge new body of work – a total of fifty-four new ballets, seventeen revivals and the dances for thirty-four operas. His teaching and choreography had a lasting influence on the classical repertoire around the world and forged an important link between the earlier age of Romantic ballet and the emerging generation of Russian dancers.

During his term at the Imperial Theatre, Petipa joined emerging Russian composer Tchaikovsky in creating the memorable masterpieces of *Swan Lake, The Nutcracker* and *The Sleeping Beauty* – the blockbuster ballets still best known to the general public. A century later, they are still central to the repertoire of all major 21st-century classical companies. It may be unimaginable to modern audiences, but *Swan Lake* was a flop when it premiered at the Bolshoi Theatre in 1877. However, by the time of Nijinsky's birth in 1890, Petipa's works had gained popularity. The premiere of *The Sleeping Beauty* that year was welcomed as an exciting new free style of ballet and a breakthrough from the previously rigid repertoire.

Around the same time in the 1840s as Petipa's arrival in Russia, Italian ballet master Filippo Taglioni was making his mark at the Teatr Weikli in Poland. Poland during the middle of the 19th century was under the control of Russia, and the visit of Taglioni's famous ballerina daughter, Marie, had a lasting impact on the culture of both countries. However, ballet in Poland was slow to acquire the same respectability as in Russia. Nevertheless, it was an influence on the young Thomas Nijinsky, known as Fomo to his Russian friends, and the Bereda sisters, Stephanie and Eleonora.

Both were drawn to ballet but were from different strata of society: Thomas was from a fourth-generation family of performers where the art and technique of dancing were handed down from father to son in the same way as an Australian Aboriginal dancer answered 21st-century choreographer Jiri Kylian's question of why he danced: "Because my father taught me and I will teach it to my son."

Stephanie and Eleonora were forbidden from dancing by their family, who believed it to be a socially unacceptable profession.

However as ballet was gradually gaining respect in Russia, it was declining in Western Europe. In France, it had deteriorated from the courtly art of Vestris's heyday during the previous century to a low-grade entertainment as earlier regarded in Russia and still then in Poland – the soft pornography of the day. The grand entertainment of kings had been reduced to a tawdry display of pretty women and, in England, was relegated to music halls. The ballet theatre had mostly become the preserve of elderly gentlemen, who wandered around the theatre at whim, entertaining their favourite dancers. It is easy to see, in retrospect, why Nijinsky was such a revelation in the early years of the next century, as male dancers were considered only accessories; they had been downgraded from their lauded status of the previous century to be tolerated only as a foil for the ballerina. In some ballets, they had disappeared altogether. In *Coppelia*, for instance, the leading male role of Franz was often performed by a woman in male costume, *en travesti* – as in opera.

Although ballet in Russia at the turn of the century held far higher status than in France, it was preserved by the wealth of the imperial regime and, towards the end of Petipa's long-term leadership, had become very conservative and stultified. Much as Pepita is revered today as the creator of the grand classical story ballets, he resisted any alteration to his institutions at the Imperial Theatre and fostered artists long after they had passed their prime. The company and general ballet environment had become ripe for reform.

FAMILY AND CHILDHOOD

Moving on to 1988, I was taken aback by the beauty of the Odesa National Academic Theatre of Opera and Ballet, Ukraine, at number 1 Tchaikovsky Street while on tour with the Australian Ballet in the tourist town of Odesa on the Black Sea.

Ukraine was still part of the Soviet Union, and the city was desperately in need of a coat of paint. It was a travesty for the city that was known as the second Paris during the 19th century. However, the theatre stood out as an architectural gem – a stunning circular Italian baroque-style palace, similar to the Paris Opera, built to replace the original theatre, which was destroyed by fire in 1873. The pleasing proportions of the auditorium and foyer are richly decorated with chandeliers and rococo niches featuring gilt busts of Russian composers and writers and Shakespearean and mythological statuary.

It was probably on this lavish new stage that the dashing young Thomas Nijinsky became infatuated with Eleonora Bereda.

They were both performing with Josef Yakovlevich Setov's Russian Opera Enterprise in the1880s. Thomas Nijinsky was a riveting bravura dancer. He came from a family of Polish revolutionaries and was skilled at regional character roles. At twenty-two years old, he was charismatic and impetuous. He thrilled the Odesa audiences with his fiery performances – particularly, his breathtaking leap.

It is hard to imagine him conforming to the discipline of the Theatrical Ballet School of the Teatr Wielki in Warsaw, the highly regarded institution where he had trained, which supplied many of the dancers for Russian private and provincial opera theatres. Offstage, his behaviour was wild and unpredictable.

The Bereda sisters attended the same school, although they were doing so in secret. They had been orphaned at an early age and brought up by their strict older brothers. The brothers did not approve of ballet, which was still deemed a dubious profession. Stephanie and Eleonora were attracted to the art form and somehow managed to take lessons at the ballet school without their brothers knowing. They were able to take part in several performances before their brothers found out. They were in deep trouble, ostracised for shaming the family and forbidden to continue.

Maybe they had a sympathetic housekeeper or nanny, for a year later, the girls managed to return to the school. Stephanie excelled and was offered a contract by the City Opera Theatre of Kyiv at the early age of 13. Nevertheless, she refused to take it up without her sister, so as soon as Eleonora turned 12, both girls left home.

They toured with the company for several years, but despite their love of ballet and the satisfaction of performing, the romance soon abated. They found it a hazardous and uncertain life. When Eleonora became engaged to a Russian cavalry officer in 1842, she was ready to forsake her career.

But a few days before the wedding, her fiancé made some disparaging remarks about Poles that seriously upset her. Eleonora broke off the engagement and vowed to never marry a Russian.

It was a limiting vow for a young girl, but eight years later, she met a handsome countryman – the dashing Thomas Nijinsky. He was madly smitten, yet Eleonora wavered when he proposed to her. She was reluctant to marry someone younger and harboured doubts about the stability of his character. Thomas persisted. One day, he suddenly announced that he was proposing to her for the last time and pulled out a revolver and threatened to kill himself if she didn't accept.

Eleonora capitulated and took on married life with Thomas, although it was not the end of her career as she hoped. She was forced to keep on touring as they needed the money. Their first child Stanislav (Stassik) was born in 1887 and Vaslav probably in 1890 – although accounts of Vaslav's birth vary from 1888–1890 – in Kyiv in the Caucasus region of Russia, where they were performing at the time.

There was no tenure or fixed salary for dancers at the time, and the birth of a second child must have added a lot of extra pressure to the family. In order to supplement their income, Thomas took on the extra role of ballet master, but it must have been a struggle bringing up a family on tour.

Although patriotic Poles, Eleonora and Thomas found it more lucrative to stay in Russia, touring with regional dance companies and circuses, than to return to Poland, where ballet was still not a paying proposition. The young Vaslav therefore grew up feeling more Russian than Pole and thought of himself as Russian for the rest of his life.

Nurtured in such a cradle of theatre, it was hardly surprising that both boys learnt to dance as naturally as learning to walk. They often danced with their father in regional dances such as the Lezginka – at which Thomas excelled.

Vaslav made his first public performance with his eldest brother at the age of five, dancing the part of a girl in the Ukrainian *hopak* at a children's performance in Odesa.

As Vaslav's dancing developed, the family was delighted to discover he had inherited his father's leap due to an elongated Achilles tendon. He had also inherited Thomas's talent for characterisation.

Two years after Vaslav's birth, Eleonora and Thomas had a third child – and only daughter. Eleonora gave birth to Bronislava in Minsk an hour after she had danced at the opera theatre. Although a talented dancer herself, Eleonora's career was finally forced to a close: with three small children and little help, there was no choice. In contrast to theatre life, staying at home with the children was cheerless and lonely. It was a constant financial struggle, and Thomas was mostly away on tour.

Disaster struck when Stassik was two years old. He fell out of the third-floor window of their home. Miraculously, he had no broken bones and appeared to make a complete recovery but was disturbingly slow at school. The tragedy was a serious setback for the family, and caring for him was an extra strain on Eleonora. Eventually, it became clear that Stassik was permanently handicapped and incapable of leading a normal life. Eleonora was no longer able to look after him adequately. She reluctantly placed him in a psychiatric institution, where he spent the rest of his life.

Eleonora was the backbone of the family, but coping alone with little support was an increasing strain. Thomas was ever the volatile charmer, living by the moment and perpetually away on tour. Gradually, he became estranged from them, formed a relationship with another dancer and severed himself from their life.

Thomas's leave-taking dramatically altered their lives. Eleonora was forced to move the family to St Petersburg and resorted to teaching ballet herself. The separation was a shattering blow to the young Vaslav – a shy and sensitive child, who did not relate easily to other children. He was deeply affected by his father's betrayal, which had a devastating and lasting effect on his psyche. From then on, he masked most of his feelings and turned all his love and affection to his mother, brother and sister.

When it became apparent that Stassik was unable to realise his performing potential, Eleonora urged the eight-year-old Vaslav to focus on his dancing. After the vicissitudes of her own career, she had set her heart on her children securing their futures through the Imperial Ballet School and Imperial Theatre, funded personally by the tsar.

Consequently, at the tender age of nine, the young Vaslav was escorted by his hopeful mother through the portals of the imposing colonnaded building of the Imperial Theatre School on the aptly named Theatre Street (now renamed Rossi Street, after its Italian architect) to audition for entry. As he began the formal, required audition exercises, the judiciary panel took note – particularly the *premier danseurs*, Nicholas Legat and his brother Sergei. The ordinary-looking boy showed a very impressive talent.

THE IMPERIAL SCHOOL

Years later, I climb the worn, steep steps to the Imperial Ballet School in Nijinsky's footsteps into the impressive Georgian-style building, now the Vaganova Institute, behind the Alexandrinsky (now Pushkin) Theatre of St Petersburg.

Much to Eleonora's joy, her son was granted a place at the esteemed establishment. It was the epitome of her dreams. She had happily plundered her meagre funds to equip him with the required uniform. He was effectively entering the services of the tsar and the uniform was of a military cadet. He wore a grey woollen shirt and trousers, a wide buckled belt, high-topped boots and a blue cap with the silver lyre insignia of the Imperial Theatrical School on the visor.

For the actual classes, the boys changed into a flowing white shirt and grey trousers. The girls' uniform was far less flamboyant: a demure brown ankle-length day dress with a long-sleeved blouse, a white fichu collar and a black apron, and a simple grey dress for class.

The timelessness of the building makes it easy to picture him flaunting his elaborate new garb as he proudly mounted the steps to begin his classes. They were embarking on eight years of rigidly disciplined study, the first two as day pupils on a trial basis, and the following six years as boarders. I see them at the barre in the bare rehearsal studio, deserted now during the holidays of the Vaganova students, rigidly fulfilling their routine class, their demeanour serious, focusing on the correct steps and avoiding the ballet master's stern stick.

Nijinsky's name is up as one of the Academy's esteemed graduates. I look harder and I can see him at the barre – his stocky figure, Tatar features, deadpan expression, focusing on the exercises, oblivious of the other students. I picture him striving towards perfection alongside the current Vaganova students 12 hours a day, 6 days a week.

I am disappointed not to find any other evidence of the great Nijinsky's years here. I scan the walls for signs of his scratched name. Two dancer-looking people escort me into a small anteroom near the entrance to show me a huge, rather vulgar, flat bronze sculpture of Nijinsky as the Faun. Not what I am looking for, but I am distracted by the eminence of the Academy building.

Still one of the world's leading ballet schools after two and a half centuries, nowadays, about 75 teachers coach about 300 students chosen annually out of 3000. As in Nijinsky's day, the audition process is still based on aptitude, physical and artistic qualities, to assess the candidate's proportions, height of jump, degree of turnout, general appearance, musicality, rhythm, coordination and artistic potential.

Then, as now, it was a monastic regime with little communication with the outside world. The thick stone walls, bare wooden floors and cold rooms are the backdrop to the singular life of novices of the religious order of the Russian Dance Theatre.

There was much competition among the students for the occasional calls to act as extras in the operas, ballets and theatre performances staged in the three Imperial Theatres governed by the Directorate: the Mariinsky, the Alexandrinsky across the road and the Mikhailovsky.

Nijinsky was one of the lucky ones offered relief from the routine and entry to the hallowed Mariinsky stage. Within a few days of entering the school, he was called to act as an extra in crowd scenes for opera; and regularly performed as a page in ballets like *The Sleeping Beauty* and *Swan Lake.* He lived these nights in a whirl of excitement, pushing aside the exhaustion of the long hours at school for the lure of the theatre at night. The Mariinsky stage was far grander than any of the regional theatres he had known with his parents.

The perfectly proportioned horseshoe-shaped Imperial Theatre, with its ornate blue and silver décor, is an extension of the tsar's palace style. The imperial family regularly attended the performances with their court retinue – the jewelled women and elaborately decorated men creating a glamorous tableau in their central box.

I sit in the tsar's box, absorbing the flavour of this exquisite hall, dreaming of the grand nights and thrilling performances. The aristocracy in fully jewelled splendour, the protocols and performances. Best to forget the 20th-century inadequacies backstage – the crowded dressing rooms and wardrobe store.

It is a credit to the Soviet regime that this historic theatre remains intact today – and has been extended. Sitting royally beside its contemporary adjunct, the Mariinsky Concert Hall, it now sits on the site of the Set Workshops and Exhibition Pavilion of the Board of Imperial Theatres, where Nijinsky's future costumes were conceived by such illustrious theatre designers as Alexander Golovin, Konstantin Korovin and Alexandre Benois.

Performing in such grand institutions was a completely new world to Nijinsky and a total contrast to his strictly regulated life in the Boy's Division of the School. It was an isolated existence. The boys and girls were not permitted to speak to each other, although like all adolescents, of course they did – and harboured all the normal fantasies, crushes and relationships. The two sexes were only officially allowed to mix in the rehearsal room. Apart from his spasmodic escapes to the stage, such a generally repressive and non-nurturing environment must have been destructive to Nijinsky's sensitive nature.

His first teachers at the school were Mikhail Obukhov and the Legat brothers. They found Nijinsky gauche and awkward in his behaviour but were dazzled by his natural virtuosity and perfect technique in class.

Nijinsky had been exposed to a variety of forms of dance and circus from an early age and his technique was very advanced, but he also exhibited that rare talent that set him apart from the other students. He instinctively knew how to project an extra dimension into the movements. He was clearly a child prodigy and quickly became a talking point at the school.

But much of the talk was provoked by jealousy. Nijinsky's introspective character laid him open to the collective cruelty of his peers. They regarded him as dumb and boring, and he was made to suffer for his talent. In the cruel way of children, they christened him the "Little Jap" and jeered at his Mongoloid features – the dark, slanting eyes, full lips and high cheekbones of a Russian peasant. Physically, he showed no sign of the *premier danseur*, the *danseur noble* – the classical prince of the Romantic ballets such as *Swan Lake* or *Giselle*. By all accounts, he looked almost the antithesis: short and stocky, devoid of aristocratic bearing or confidence. Like many prodigies, Nijinsky found his talent to be a social impediment. He hated the fact that he was regarded with awe; it made him feel alienated from other people and blocked his development.

At nine years old, Nijinsky was shy, awkward and vulnerable; a "one-off", maybe a genius in the making, who fitted no mould or stereotype and was ill-equipped to defend himself against the constant bullying of the other boys. There was no support structure at the school for gifted children. He was continuously ostracised with taunting remarks such as, "Are you a girl, you dance so well?" The other boys prodded him in the back and forced him into acts to get him into trouble.

It was a poisonous atmosphere for Nijinsky – not the singular training in dance his mother had visualised, but more a training for withstanding the toughest forces of life. Isolated by his talent and bereft of the social skills and everyday ease to relate to others, Nijinsky must have felt as if he were in solitary confinement. His sister Bronislava was his only confidante, but he hardly ever saw her. He was incarcerated at the school, hardly ever at home and cut off from the outside world.

The isolation forced him to develop his inner resources. Nijinsky focused on his creative development, working hard in the classroom and studio. He discovered the school's library of books and lost himself in the world of ideas to offset his loneliness and boredom. He confided to his sister that it was only when he was dancing that he felt free.

In 1901, during his third year, a gang of boys played a terrible trick on him. They erected a barrier in the studio using a heavy wooden music stand, which they dared Nijinsky to jump over. As he ran towards it, one of the boys rubbed soap on the floor to make it slippery, and another raised the barrier higher. Nijinsky hit the barrier at full force and crashed to the floor, seriously injuring his abdomen. He was in a coma for several days and, when he did emerge, was still in danger of lasting damage from the severe physical and psychological trauma. After several months of hospitalisation, he was eventually declared fit enough in mind and body to resume normal life.

When he returned to the school the following year, Nijinsky's academic performance had slipped, although he continued to score well in the physical and creative subjects, which did not require verbal skills. Despite his extraordinary talent in dance, Nijinsky's future was now in jeopardy. He was warned that he would be expelled unless he improved his conduct and achieved higher marks in his general studies. Although he had started school as a diligent student, Nijinsky was so affected by his social misery that he only hung on to his place through the high standard of his dancing.

The shocking experience of the accident did not deter his attempts to win the other boys' approval. If anything, it renewed his determination. He wrote in his diary that he played a lot of pranks—that made him popular.

It was not long before his efforts backfired. Nijinsky was one of a group firing wads of paper with slingshots out of their carriage windows on the way to the theatre when one of the shots hit the hat of a passerby, who unfortunately happened to be a government official. Although the culprit could have been in any one of the three carriages, the other boys framed the star pupil – Nijinsky. He had been sitting by the open window, and they figured had he was less likely to come to harm. They were grossly mistaken. Given his track record, Nijinsky was in serious trouble. He was expelled from the school, much to Eleonora's devastation – she wept for two days before desperately imploring one of the school inspectors, Vladimir Pisnyachevsky, to intercede on her son's behalf. Both he and Nijinsky's teachers pleaded with the director of the Imperial Theatre, Vladimir Telyakovsky, who finally agreed to lighten Nijinsky's punishment by expelling him from the boarding establishment and forcing him to return all uniforms and books supplied by the school. It was a cruel punishment – Nijinsky was outlawed and forced to feel even more apart from the other pupils. He was further humiliated by having to wear a tatty second-hand uniform, which was all Eleonora could muster, in an establishment where pride in appearance was paramount. But more disastrously for his struggling family, his school stipend was cancelled. Luckily, after a month of torture, Nijinsky was pardoned, released and allowed to return to the school on the same basis as everyone else.

I stand in the central St Petersburg street opposite the house I have been directed to by the Mariinsky archivist. The unassuming Georgian terrace is purported to be where Nijinsky lived with his family, but there is no plaque or sign of confirmation. The ballet company is on holiday, and It has taken days to extract the information. My faithful driver assures me this is the right place, but we are both running out of energy after a frustrating Nijinsky-chasing day. I focus on summoning up Nijinsky as Tamara instructed me. I picture him sitting out his punishment with his head bowed in misery around the table with Eleonora and Bronislava, but is it my imagination or a melding of time and place?

FOKINE

Nijinsky was back in full physical form by the time of the school examinations, where he made such an impression on Mikhail Fokine – who was one of the examiners – that he was late for his next class.

Fokine was both a leading dancer of the Imperial Theatre and a teacher at the school – a tall, good-looking, charismatic and popular personality, who was just beginning to be noticed as a choreographer. It was the first time he had seen Nijinsky dance, and he was so carried away with enthusiasm that he broke the strictly formal class structure and raved about him to Nijinsky's sister, Bronislava, who happened to be in his class.

Much to Eleonora's joy, Bronislava had followed her brother to the school. She had also inherited her father's elongated Achilles tendon and was showing signs of similar talent.

Bronislava explains in her biography how astonished she was when Fokine told her, in front of the other pupils, "We have given other students the mark of 12, but there has never been anyone who danced like Nijinsky ... I would have given him a 20 or even a 30. He surpassed anything we have ever seen before . . . wonderful."

It was music to the ears of Bronislava, Nijinsky's closest friend and supporter, the one person he admitted to his inner life.

Rumours of the quiet student's sensational dancing in the examinations ricocheted around the Imperial Theatre, and the other dancers began turning up at Nijinsky's classes to check him out for themselves. Another promising young dancer, the dark-haired, serious Tamara Karsavina, noticed Nijinsky for the first time in the classroom during exercises for elevation. In her later life, she recalled the impact of the small, undistinguished boy who rose cleanly off the floor when he jumped, well above the heads and shoulders of his taller classmates. Little did she realise at the time that they would be paired in the history of dance – that she would become the small boy's major partner and co-star in a future, freer style of ballet company – the illustrious Ballets Russes.

Fokine was frustrated with the stagnant state of ballet at the Imperial Theatre, the Mariinsky, and was longing to implement new ideas. In desperation, he wrote a formal letter to the Directorate of the Imperial Theatre, outlining his ideas. It was a risky step for him to take within such a rigid regime, but there are no reports of it damaging his status. Nor did it result in any immediate changes. Fokine had to bide his time until the following year when he encountered the two reformers who became the dominant influences of his career. It was due to their freethinking influence that he became a choreographer of great importance in developing an individual style that liberated dance from its court confines.

Fokine was captivated by the new philosophy of realism that Konstantin Stanislavsky was pioneering at the Moscow Arts Theatre, the Stanislavsky Method still practised by actors of the 21st century. It inspired him to find a way of reflecting the free world sought by the growing numbers of pre-Revolutionary activists in Russia on the ballet stage.

Fokine's choreographic language was transformed by the influence of radical American dancer Isadora Duncan. Duncan was an alternative artist, not a classically trained dancer, who advocated naturalism and responded emotionally to the music with apparently spontaneous, natural, free-flowing movements. On her first visit to Russia at the end of 1904, she exposed Fokine to an entirely new way of interpreting dance.

Duncan was the first choreographer to bring out the meaning of music in dance: to alter the direction of dance from pure movement to movement expressing sound. Fokine was also captivated by her Hellenic theme. At a time when the theatre was cluttered with ornate clothing and courtly etiquette, Duncan styled herself as the spiritual daughter of classical Greece. She dressed in long, flowing, white Grecian toga-like garments and bare feet.

Although not a revolutionary like Duncan, Fokine was fired with her revolutionary zeal. He found it refreshingly pure and authentic. Duncan was radical in almost every aspect of her life – both on and off stage. Her individuality inspired Fokine to find a way of liberating choreography from its stiff, unnatural forms and patterns: to replace the traditional stylised (panto)mime used to relate the ballet story with a more natural form of expression and change the rigid lines of the *corps de ballet* on the stage to smaller, looser groups of soloists.

Unlike Duncan, Fokine wanted to change things within the existing framework of classical ballet. He wanted to update, not discard. Fokine's relatively natural forms and historical authenticity were the major elements of his new form of Romantic ballet.

Fokine's new style took the eye of the young arts entrepreneur, Sergei Diaghilev, with whom he had attended Duncan's performances in St Petersburg. Diaghilev took note that Fokine's new form of ballet was more natural and accessible to audiences. It fitted perfectly with his own plans of promoting Russian culture and he started to consider the possibility of taking Fokine's ballet to the wider world.

In 1906, Fokine was given the opportunity to introduce his new ideas when he was commissioned to create some dances for the graduation performance of the Imperial School. He searched the Imperial Archives for an existing authentic Greek ballet to reflect Duncan's theme, which he could use as a basis for his new work. To his delight, he discovered the libretto for *Acis and Galatea*, devised in 1896 by Lev Ivanov from Ovid's *Metamorphosis*.

During the auditions for the ballet, Fokine was annoyed when he saw that one of the group of students trying out as the faun appeared to have disobeyed his instructions. Strangely, it was the same student he had been so impressed by in the examinations. Nijinsky hovered in the air much longer than the others and landed much further away. Fokine asked him to assume the pose of a faun. Nijinsky froze. It was so convincing that Fokine decided on the spot to give him a special solo in the ballet. Nijinsky had unintentionally leapt into Fokine's choreography. His faun was the talk of the school well before the performance. It heralded the birth of a key artistic partnership – the first of many roles Fokine created for Nijinsky and a key factor in the success of the Ballets Russes.

Fokine's choreography from then on was almost always created around Nijinsky. Although a talented dancer himself, Nijinsky became the vehicle for his ideas. Despite their totally different personalities, their destinies were intertwined. In the ballet *Eunice,* his next notable choreographic development in 1907, Fokine gave Nijinsky the role of a slave – the first of many legendary slave roles that Nijinsky brought to life in Fokine's ballets.

Eunice, based on Henryk Sienkiewicz's novel *Quo Vadis,* was endorsed by a request from the *prima ballerina assoluta* of the Imperial Ballet, Mathilde Kschessinska, to perform the title role. It was tantamount to the official imperial seal of approval. *Eunice* saw the impact of another legend in the making – Anna Pavlova – in *The Dance of the Seven Veils.*

Eunice was Fokine's tribute to Duncan. At the time, the costumes were considered outrageously indecent compared to the buttoned-up artifice of previous ballets. In a radical move towards the freedom of Duncan's bare feet and minimum or lack of clothing today, Fokine had the *corps de ballet* dancing in tights painted with toes to look like bare feet.

However, the ballet that marked Duncan's most direct influence on classical ballet was Fokine's *Chopiniana,* orchestrated by Glazenov. His ideas had been sparked by Duncan's *Chopin Waltz.* Nijinsky was the only male dancer in *Chopiniana* –a poet surrounded by a throng of sylphs. Fokine later developed *Chopiniana* into the now-classic *Les Sylphides.*

When Alexandre Benois, one of the artistic advisers to the Director of the Imperial Theatre, suggested the idea for a ballet based on a 17th-century Gobelin tapestry, Fokine created *Le Gobelin Anime* for Nijinsky's graduation, and the role of Armida's Page –

the White Slave – specifically for him. It was Fokine's first choreography for the Imperial Theatre stage, which would eventually lead to his appointment as the first chief choreographer of Diaghilev's Ballets Russes and a major contributor to its early success. He was invited to develop *Le Gobelin Anime* into a larger work – *Le Pavillon d'Armide,* for the company's groundbreaking first season in Paris.

DEBUT

The professional theatre debut of the *Wunderkind* Nijinsky took place while he was still at the Imperial School. Nijinsky was amazed himself in 1906 when he was chosen to perform with the established artists of the Imperial Ballet for the 150th anniversary of Mozart's death. He was sixteen years old and a year and a half from his graduation. It was an unheard-of occurrence in the rigidly disciplined Imperial Theatre regime for a student to partner with the ballerina, Vera Trefilova, particularly on such an auspicious occasion. He was to feature with four ballerinas and three *premier danseurs* in the *Roses and Butterflies* ballet, choreographed by Nicolas Legat for the opera, *Don Giovanni.*

Nijinsky's selection was primarily due to the Legat brothers – his first teacher/admirers at the school. He was gaining a reputation for his perfect classical technique, but this performance with Trefilova mesmerised the audience – it was the first public indication of his extraordinary stage presence.

In everyday life, Nijinsky merged with the crowd and, in rehearsal, worked mechanically, perfecting the movements without any show of expression, but once onstage, he appeared to metamorphose into the role. He was that character, thinking and feeling the part in rapport with the audience.

It was apparently phenomenal to observe his transformation: according to Benois, Nijinsky's stocky build, lack of physical proportion and apparent lack of capacity for intelligent thought would have disqualified him from a place at the Imperial School had he not transformed the moment he began to move in class or onstage. At the time of his debut on the Mariinsky stage, Benois's impression was that "he resembled a stock boy more than a fairy-tale hero and was so timid that he would fade into the background".

Benois describes Nijinsky as about 5 feet 8 inches fully grown, with overdeveloped thighs, calves on which the muscles protruded like coiled springs, pale skin and a perfectly ordinary Tartar face. But he says that Nijinsky projected such a strong stage presence that people perceived him to be tall.

Bronislava wrote that she thought she knew everything about her brother until the first time she saw his transformation on stage: "He radiates an inner force that, by its very radiance, envelops the theatre. Establishing his art became, for me, a dancing discovery: seeing him dance, I was filled with awe, captivated by his art."

Such extraordinary raves continued. A few days after his sensational premiere with Trefilova, Nijinsky partnered Pavlova – another rising talent – for the second performance of the anniversary opera. Together, Nijinsky's animated virtuosity and Pavlova's ethereal delicacy made a magical duo. Both dancers were to become household names in the Western world; both pushed the barriers of the art form and both were pivotal to the development of dance in the international arena. But individually, not together.

Shortly afterwards, the Imperial Ballet formally acknowledged Nijinsky's talent by offering him a contract in advance of his graduation. It was a great and unusual honour, yet surprisingly turned down by his mother. Eleonora thought he was not ready to enter the profession. She well understood the limitations of a dancing career and believed he needed another disciplinary year to bring his academic studies up to the same standard as his dancing.

When Nijinsky finally graduated, the company offered him the immediate rank of *coryphée*, a level above the usual first-year *corps de ballet*, with a higher rate of pay.

Tamara Karsavina was one of Nijinsky's first partners in the company. She wrote in her memoir, *Theatre Street,* of her impression of the "Eighth Wonder of the World" as the chief elf in *A Midsummer Night's Dream:*

> *He is not much to look at and never will be a first-rate mime ...the guise of a plain, unprepossessing boy fell off – a creature exotic, feline, elfin, completely eclipsed the respectable comeliness, the dignified commonplace of conventional virility. Special dances were constantly introduced for Nijinsky; I was almost invariably his partner.*

It was a partnership that shaped the history of ballet. They first performed a *pas de deux* from an old Petipa ballet *Roxana,* but Nijinsky and Kasarvina first attracted serious notice for their bravura and synchronicity as a couple when they performed the peasant *pas de deux* – the "party piece" of *Giselle.*

As a teenager now, Nijinsky was developing his inner personality and experimenting with his external image – for a time, he sported a moustache. He read Tolstoy, Dickens and Dostoevsky and was absorbed by music, playing several instruments himself, including the piano.

It was an unsettling time in Russia, with reform rife inside and outside the ballet world. Nijinsky experienced the seeds of revolution first hand on Bloody Sunday – 9 January 1905 – the horrific, historic day, which was the precursor to the deposing of the Romanov regime and destruction of the Russian Empire.

In October of that year, Nijinsky was caught in a terror-stricken crowd being charged by Cossacks on horseback, on his way back from the theatre with a group of other students. They ventured out again later to help look for the missing sister of one of the other students. Rumour has it that a red flag was thrust into their hands, which placed them in jeopardy, as they were dressed in their uniforms of the tsar. The sister was never found and Nijinsky was wounded by a lash on the forehead from a Cossack whip. He bore that scar for the rest of his life, both on his forehead and in his psyche. It evoked a lifelong loathing of war and conflict – reflecting strongly on his radical choreography and the writing in his diary.

The horror was spreading within his world. Revolt against the rigidly ruled Imperial Directorate was brewing within the Theatre. Fired by the influence of his teacher Sergei Legat, who was among the group of reformists, Nijinsky was among the throng of students and staff at a disastrous, stormy meeting.

The reform group were demanding the return of Petipa and the rights to their management, including the improvement of education, instruction in theatrical make-up, permission for the graduating students to smoke, and permission for the advanced students to wear their own shoes and starched collars and cuffs under their school jackets.

To cement their intent, they called a strike of the next day's performance. The revolt failed, and the passionate Legat slashed his throat.

It was devasting news to Nijinsky. Legat was his major role model and mentor – partly substituting for his father. Together with his brother Nicholas, who had taken over from Petipa as the chief choreographer of the Imperial Theatre, Legat had played a large part in Nijinsky's early success. He had groomed him and acted as his protector. Bronislava asserts in her memoirs that Legat and Nijinsky's other early teacher, Obukhov, several times saved her brother from harsh punishment.

The blow of the suicide was deepened by talk that Legat's aging lover, Marie Petipa, daughter of the great ballet master, had persuaded him to revolt.

Publicly, Nijinsky's profile was growing. He was becoming attractive to the aristocracy of St Petersburg, who were always on the lookout for new talent to patronise. He was favoured to appear more often on stage.

KSCHESSINSKA

After his illustrious debut in *Roses and Butterflies*, the young Nijinsky was in constant demand as a partner to the senior ballerinas. The leading artists of the Mariinsky – Olga Preobrajenska; Liubov Egorova; Vera Trefilova and Anna Pavlova; as well as *prima ballerina assoluta* Mathilde Kschessinska, who was a powerful personage in the Imperial Theatres and at court, all sought him out. Kschessinska had been a favourite at the Imperial Theatre for twenty years. She was mistress to the tsar before his marriage and to other members of the imperial family, publicly acknowledged as the "mistress of the St Petersburg Ballet."

A Pole herself, like Nijinsky, Kschessinska was a vivacious and thrilling dancer, although not a great technician. She relied on theatrical craft and cliches to disguise her shortcomings and worked hard at perfecting her pirouettes, which never failed to excite her fans.

Kschessinska was regarded as the embodiment of a Petipa classical ballerina, the image of the great star of the Imperial Theatre, said to "stir the emotions." She was always aware of performing as the "Ballerina", keeping centrestage, well in front of the *corps de ballet*. She also resorted to exotic stunts such as performing with a live (drugged) snake in the ballet *La Bayadere* and kept a goat for her appearances in *Esmeralda*.

Such was the relationship between the imperial family and its Theatre that Kschessinska captivated the young *tsarevich* on her first performance. It led to an alliance that had a bearing on the rest of her life and a significant impact on the Imperial Theatre.

A few years later, when he married and inherited the ill-fated Romanov throne, Tsar Nicholas was dutifully forced to relinquish his intimate relationship with Kschessinska. He placed her under the protection of his uncle, the Grand Duke Sergei Mikhailovich. Kschessinska then presided over an entourage of Romanov Grand Duke cousins – known for most of their lives as the "Young Boys," and was later accepted by the imperial family as the mistress of Grand Duke Andrei Vladimirovich, the tsar's nephew and an official at court, with whom she had a child and later married in exile in Paris after the revolution.

Kschessinska's engrossing domestic life made her reluctant to perform outside the country, but her personality; talent and connections made her a dominating force in ballet in Russia. Kschessinska was the adored darling of the St Petersburg public. For over a quarter of a century, they followed her several farewell performances and subsequent returns to the stage. She was showered with jewels, houses and other symbols of wealth. With the ballet company, Kschessinska was not a person to be trifled with: she took full advantage of her privileged position and had no hesitation in calling on her imperial connections for casting demands and other such issues.

Unprecedented approval was granted for a celebration of her tenth anniversary with the Imperial Theatre, for instance – traditionally only given after twenty years. To be chosen to dance with the dazzling and influential Mathilde was the ultimate seal of approval: her usual partner was Nicolas Legat – the *premier danseur* of the company, but she was taken with Nijinsky after performing *La fille mal gardée* with him in 1907. Like Margot Fonteyn with Rudolf Nureyev in later years, Kschessinska found it revitalising to dance with a rising star in the sunset of her career. She invited Nijinsky to dance with her on many prestigious occasions, including the farewell benefit performance for Maria Petipa at the Mariinsky in 1907.

Petipa was renowned for creating the role of the Lilac Fairy in her father's classic creation, *The Sleeping Beauty.* Kschessinska and Nijinsky were a highlight of the farewell evening with their *divertissement – Nocturne* by Chopin, choreographed specially for the occasion. Kschessinska next invited Nijinsky to partner with her in *Le Pavillon d'Armide* – from which she later resigned and was replaced by Pavlova. But she was very offended at a later date (a benefit performance in 1910, celebrating her twenty years as an artist) when Nijinsky turned down her offer. When she heard that he had danced with Pavlova shortly after, she refused to accept his explanation of needing more time to get into shape and vowed that she would have him out of the company – and his sister, too.

There was growing rivalry between Kschessinska and Pavlova, who had eclipsed her as a lyrical dancer. Both ballerinas were individual artists who refused to sacrifice their artistic freedom or status. Kschessinska was not beholden to the Directorate of the Imperial Theatre because of her exalted connections; Pavlova preferred to shape her own career, away from the confines of the Directorate or impresario/dictators such as Diaghilev.

Although Nijinsky was a good partner, female stars were not always happy with the result. He unintentionally stole their stardom. No matter how wonderful their performance, Nijinsky naturally dominated the stage and was almost always the focus of both the applause and the reviews.

Kschessinska had her own reasons for "nurturing" the rising star, but many of his other partners were frequently frustrated and some – such as the great Pavlova – refused to dance with him more than a few times. She openly objected to Nijinsky stealing the limelight: it was a great loss to the public to mostly miss their magic on stage. When Pavlova and Nijinsky danced the Bluebird *divertissement* from *La Belle au bois dormant (The Sleeping Beauty)* together, it was perceived to be poetry in motion – the epitome of perfect artistry.

Nijinsky was such a natural performer that he was oblivious to competition; his only intent was to improve his performance. His social isolation made him a relentless disciplinarian, spending hours in rehearsal each day.

LVOV

It was only a matter of time before Nijinsky's dancing attracted the attention of the St Petersburg elite – the set of dilettantes who regarded all of Europe as their playground. Nijinsky was approached by Prince Pavel Lvov, Chamberlain of His Royal Highness and secretary of the Minister of Transport and Communications. Lvov was in his early thirties, six feet tall, homosexual and distinctly aristocratic in appearance. He was a patron of many sports and athletic organisations and could have met Nijinsky through Mikhail Fokine's brother, Alexandre, who was a champion sportsman, but it was more likely to have been through certain contacts within the company who arranged such liaisons. Lvov made his move at the premiere of *Le Pavillon d'Armide.* Nijinsky was elated with the enthusiastic reaction from the audience for his performance of Armida's page; he was young and impressionable, a serious artist in his first year at the Imperial Theatre.

During an interval, he was handed a note of invitation from Lvov to join a group dining together after the show.

It was a turning point in Nijinsky's life. The relationship with Lvov allowed him to develop a sense of belonging: he became more confident and concerned about his appearance. Lvov introduced him to St Petersburg society, to the sophisticated delights of restaurants and nightclubs and to the homosexual culture, which was tolerated at the time, although not openly approved.

It was, strangely, a relationship of which his mother thoroughly approved. Eleonora was worried that Nijinsky would become a womaniser like his father and was impressed by the prince's courtesy and consideration for the family. Whether or not it was naivete, she saw the liaison with Lvov as compensation for her son's lack of a compassionate father. On the practical front, Lvov also offered a much-needed means of financial support.

Nijinsky's initiation into the homosexual world, with its jealousies and sensitivities, may have contributed to his eventual downfall. Although ripe for a protector, he appeared to be naturally attracted to girls.

His first girlfriend had been Liza, the daughter of a seamstress who lived on the floor below the family apartment. He had various other flirtations and attractions including Tonya (the sister of Olga Chumakova, the personal partner of Nikolas Legat), whom he got into trouble by sending a note to the school. Then at the age of eighteen, he declared he was going to marry Maria Gorshkova, whom he had partnered for her graduation. His mother warned him that Gorshkova was ambitious for her career, but Nijinsky was devastated when Maria asked him to promise to insist on dancing with her in his next *pas de deux* while she was in his arms one day. It was a rude shock that deepened his mistrust of other people's motives and left him ripe for plucking by the other sex – particularly an older, wiser, role model like Lvov.

Prince Lvov funded Nijinsky's development. Nijinsky was able to give up the teaching of social dancing to private pupils, which he only tolerated in an effort to supplement his support to the family. He was constantly worried about his mother's poverty and implored the Directorate to let him dance more often, as they were paid according to their number of performances. Lvov's patronage allowed him to take lessons himself with the legendary Italian ballet master Enrico Cecchetti, who had been working in St Petersburg since the 1890s – first at the Imperial Theatre and now with private pupils. Cecchetti operated in the traditional, now stylised manner of a ballet master – thumping his stick and screaming and shouting in a mixture of French, Italian and Russian.

The liaison with Lvov lasted less than a year but bolstered his confidence and education. Among the other lines of growth and development, it opened Nijinsky up to explore his sexuality. He writes in his diary of giving up "the sin" of masturbation, which was thought at the time to have depleted energy. All this time, Nijinsky admits in his diary, he was looking for approval.

Although he had many opportunities to perform, and was acclaimed by audiences, he was sensitive to the reaction of the other dancers and reluctant to inflame their envy. It was so exaggerated in his mind that he later reflected in his diary that he was "no longer cheerful, because I felt death. I was afraid of people and used to lock myself in my room."

In order to cheer himself up, Nijinsky allowed his fellow company dancer friend Anatole Bourman to persuade him to experiment with visiting a prostitute. To his total embarrassment, he almost immediately contacted gonorrhoea. He was mortified and depressed throughout a long illness. Luckily, he was still supported by Lvov, who nurtured him and paid for his nursing and medicines.

DIAGHILEV

It was Lvov who introduced Nijinsky to Diaghilev. Diaghilev had been watching Nijinsky for some time, admiring him from afar, but was jolted into taking serious notice when he saw him perform as the pampered White Slave in *Le Pavillon d'Armide* – Fokine's ballet reviving the elaborate Rococo art of Fontainebleau and Versailles. He was not the first prospective suitor Lvov had introduced: Nijinsky believed that Lvov "forced me to be unfaithful to him with Diaghilev because he thought Diaghilev would be useful to me". We well know he was right: Diaghilev had big plans for Nijinsky personally and professionally – he had decided he needed Nijinsky's talent for the Russian ballet seasons he was planning in Europe. Nijinsky was at a vulnerable stage, having discovered an escape from poverty and isolation in the imperial regime through his relationship with Lvov.

Years later, when he was writing his diary, Nijinsky described his state since his graduation from the school the year before: "I was let out. I felt free, but the freedom terrified me." He was seventeen; Diaghilev was thirty-four. But his feelings towards Diaghilev at the time are difficult to fathom. Nijinsky writes disparagingly of approaching the relationship solely from a mercenary point of view:

> *I hated him for his voice, which was too self assured, but I went in search of luck. I found luck there because I immediately made love to him. I trembled like an aspen leaf. I hated him, but I put up a pretence, for I knew that my*

> *mother and I would starve to death. I understood Diaghilev from the first moment and therefore pretended that I agreed with all his views. I realised one had to live, and therefore it did not matter to me what sacrifice I made.*

Nijinsky's instincts told him if he were to leave Diaghilev, he would starve to death, "because he was not mature enough for life".

It was the first clue that Nijinsky was not exclusively homosexual, a fact that is normally overlooked because of the influence of Diaghilev. Historically, Nijinsky's name is inseparable from that of Diaghilev – the colourful and cultured Russian impresario, whose entrepreneurship enriched Western arts and laid the foundation for ballet in the 21st century.

It is no secret that Nijinsky and Diaghilev were lovers and that the early success of Diaghilev's Ballets Russes was built on the talent of his star. It was a relationship that appeared to be unequal, but Diaghilev and Nijinsky needed each other more than others were aware.

Much has been written of the powerful personality of Diaghilev: without Diaghilev, the Western world may not have heard the music of Stravinsky; the choreography of Balanchine; the dancing of Nijinsky, Tamara Karsavina and Marie Rambert (both she and the other founder of British Ballet, Ninette de Valois, started their dancing careers in his Ballets Russes) and later, Leonide Massine, Anton Dolin and Serge Lifar. Without the innovation of the Ballets Russes, we may not have seen Picasso, Braque and Cocteau's theatre designs. Diaghilev introduced the great Rimsky-Korsakov to Western Europe and gave licence to Prokofiev and many other major Russian, and later, European, composers.

French choreographer Angelin Preijocaj said in recent times that it is the responsibility of 21st-century choreographers to carry on Diaghilev's adventure – his exploration of the possibilities of expression in dance. Although not an artist himself, Diaghilev had the rare gift of bringing creative people together and drawing out their talents.

The risks he took in the theatre are seldom seen today.

But Diaghilev would never have had the same impact without Nijinsky: it was their liaison that shaped the future of dance and spawned a whole new epoch of creativity. The inspired impresario and artistic genius together opened the window of Russian culture to the West and exposed it to new influences.

Nijinsky's relationship with Diaghilev was the most formative of his life, but in contrast to his mentor's flamboyant style, little is known of Nijinsky's personality, despite the fact that his performances have been documented in detail. Throughout his life, Nijinsky kept mostly to himself. The people he was closest to were his mother Eleonora, sister Bronislava, lover Diaghilev and wife Romola. It was not until his diary was published by Romola in 1936 that the public had a glimpse into his mind.

Diaghilev was an impressive figure, solidly built and calculatingly distinguished in appearance, with a distinctive white piece in the front of his dyed dark hair, which had earned him the nickname of "Chinchilla". He was an impeccable dresser; a theatrical arbiter of elegance immaculate in evening dress of white shirt, tie and tails, powdered and perfumed; he sported a monocle, which he was unlikely to need, and carried a Malacca cane with a silver top. He had a nasal voice and a horror of cats. He had inherited his excessive superstitiousness from his serf-born nannie, who presided over the *samovar* of his St Petersburg salon. He refused to be photographed and believed that he would lose money if anyone placed his hat on the table.

Although initially discounted culturally as the country cousin (from his family estate at Perm, near the Ural Mountains), Diaghilev had been reared on the regular concerts and literary evenings of his grandfather's house from an early age. He had developed a sound musical knowledge and cultural curiosity. He had extensive piano-playing skills and was fluent in French and German. Diaghilev was more inclined as a dandy and more grandiose than the rest of his intellectual circle. He was regal in manner and formal in speech. As time went by, his fastidiousness, theatrical style, fur-lined coat and aloofness created the illusion of a distant royalty.

Diaghilev first became widely known in the cultural circles in St Petersburg as the editor and publisher of *Mir Iskusstva* ("World of Art"), the first quality art magazine in Russia. Diaghilev had devised the magazine with his group of intellectual friends, including artists Alexander Benois (whose architect father had built the Mariinsky and St Petersburg Bolshoi theatres) and Leon Rosenberg – who took his grandfather's name of Bakst – writer Walter Nouvel and his cousin and lover Dmitri (known as Dima) Filosofov, who was literary editor of the magazine. Filosofov had introduced him to the "Pickwickians" – the rather arrogant young circle devoted to promoting the artistic values and classical tradition of 18th century St Petersburg – and had initially "culturally educated" the country cousin.

By the time he created *Mir Iskusstva*, Diaghilev had more than compensated for his early cultural isolation: he had undertaken the traditional 19th-century "grand tour" of Europe several times and was familiar with the cultural life of all of Europe and its identities. He had met the writer Oscar Wilde and artist Aubrey Beardsley, who featured regularly in the magazine, and was a friend of Tchaikovsky and the idolised Russian poet Pushkin's son, Grigori. The now "educated" Diaghilev had assumed leadership of the Pickwickians and was considered one of the up-and-coming figures in the arts. He was held in good regard by the tsar's uncle, Grand Duke Vladimir, a highly cultivated man who was president of the Imperial Academy of the Arts, which was in charge of all the artistic institutions of the country.

When a friend and relative of the circle – the progressive-thinking Prince Sergei Mikhail Volkonsky – was appointed to the key position of Director of the Imperial Theatres, Diaghilev was appointed as a junior director in charge of special projects. He was given the responsibility of editing the annual report of the Imperial Theatres – a rather dull, statistical publication that recorded performances at the subsidised theatres in St Petersburg and Moscow and provided lists of the companies and principal dancers, singers and actors. As in all his endeavours, the naturally entrepreneurial Diaghilev put aesthetic values ahead of economic concerns and upgraded the yearbook to a deluxe publication along the lines of *Mir Iskusstva*, with the help of his talented friends, although he ran 50% over budget. Nevertheless, he was congratulated by everyone, including the tsar, for producing a book of exceptional elegance.

Diaghilev's next venture was a collaborative staging of Rimsky-Korsakov's opera *Sadko* for the Imperial Theatre. He had studied music at university, including composition under Rimsky-Korsakov (who told him he would not make a composer). Diaghilev's direction of *Sadko* was considered a success by the theatre authorities, but they were upset by his radical attitude and overspending when he embarked on his next production of the ballet *Sylvia*.

Diaghilev was a true entrepreneur who saw the merit in mixing the tried and true, the top of the field, with the new. He invited the Legat brothers to choreograph and perform in the ballet and engaged emerging artists, such as the talented young Leon Bakst, to design the costumes. Diaghilev and bureaucracy were not a good mix: he inevitably upset the Directorate by assuming too much power too quickly and voicing his opinions. He was considered too much of a risk by the conservative regime, and total control of the ballet was officially taken away from him. Diaghilev was outraged by the undermining of his authority and unwisely attempted a form of blackmail by threatening to resign in umbrage from the editorship of the annual report. It immediately became a battle of wills, in which he had little chance. Diaghilev was ordered to continue editing the yearbook, which he categorically refused. His ally, Grand Duke Sergei Mikhailovich, sought reassurance from the tsar on his behalf and thought he had succeeded in gaining his support.

Both he and Diaghilev were unprepared for the shock of the announcement in the following morning's *Government Gazette*. Diaghilev was dismissed from all crown service. It was later alleged that the tsar was also shocked at the consequences of their conversation – he had told the Grand Duke, "In Diaghilev's case, I would not have resigned." It was the degree of dismissal, "according to article three," which delivered the worst damage, as article three was only applied in exceptional cases and only in connection with disreputable behaviour.

It was a major blow to Diaghilev's career – such a damming method of dismissal meant that doors would be closed to him in Russia permanently. At a later date, he had to suffer the humiliation of being removed from the theatre by police when he was invited by Benois to watch a rehearsal of *Le Pavillon d'Armide*. But it forced him to dramatically change course and turn his eyes towards the rest of the world. If it were not for the *Sylvia* scandal, Diaghilev would probably have remained in Russia and there would have been no Ballets Russes.

Undaunted, Diaghilev embarked on a series of *Mir Iskusstva* exhibitions of paintings in St Petersburg, culminating in the first representative retrospective exhibition of Russian paintings through the ages. He combed the countryside to discover ancestral works hidden on estates that, in many cases, the owners were not aware of themselves. He unearthed gems in barns and attics to put together three thousand works in the largest exhibition ever mounted in Russia, opened with a flourish by the tsar in the grand hall of the Tauride Palace, St Petersburg, in February 1905 and celebrated in Moscow by a banquet in Diaghilev's honour.

The Tauride Palace remains thrillingly beautiful – a masterpiece of aristocratic 18th-century Russian architecture, tired but still commanding. Set in a large, landscaped park complete with ponds and artificial islands on the banks of the river Neva, it must have been a fitting background for the scale and grandeur of Diaghilev's inspired exhibition. The majestic two-storeyed colonnaded building at the centre of the complex flaunts a cupola and lavishly decorated interiors with chandeliers with imperial eagles, which must have been overlooked during Soviet days. The scaled-down park now bears a large statue of Tchaikovsky at the entrance. It is busy with walkers and strollers as I circumnavigate the massive complex. The landmark exhibition, charting the entire history of Russia, caused a sensation throughout the country. It was never forgotten by those who saw it, many of whom paid more than one visit.

The outstanding success of such an ambitious endeavour prompted Diaghilev to embark on his first entrepreneurial venture outside Russia. He had long had his eye on Paris as the centre of Western art (there were reputedly more artists per square metre living in Paris at the time than in any other location in the world), and in 1906, launched his first international presentation – a similar exhibition of Russian painting and sculpture *L'Exposition de l'Art Russe* at the Salon d'Automne. It was an inspired decision. The exhibition was even more successful in Paris than the one in St Petersburg and aroused Parisian interest in Russian culture. It was the soft launch of the glittering Diaghilev era – the first of Diaghilev's series of Russian seasons in Western Europe. Ever the charming man of culture, Diaghilev made himself known to many of the key society hostesses and to fellow entrepreneur and future impresario Jewish music publisher Gabriel Astruc.

Studying Diaghilev's portrait in St Petersburg's Russian Museum, I note his careless and majestic pose and the quiet figure of his old nurse in the background underwriting the displayed description of his extraordinary personality – his energy, exquisite taste and artistic culture. It cites him as "inspired and organised" and refers to his "daring and ambitious nature".

The following year, Diaghilev introduced Russian music – his own special field of knowledge – in a series of concerts at the Paris Opera. As always, Diaghilev aimed only at offering the top talent. The six concerts offered a glimmering of the whole gamut of Russian gems: the famous bass Feodor Chaliapine made his debut singing both on his own and with great Russian soprano, Felia Litvinne; Sergei Rachmaninoff played; Rimsky-Korsakov conducted his *Christmas Eve*; Josef Hofmann played the music of Alexander Scriabin and Alexander Glazunov conducted his *Poeme Symphonique*. In 1908, Diaghilev took advantage of the swelling Paris theatre audiences of La Belle Époque (it was the heyday of Sarah Bernhardt, and half a million Parisians attended the theatre at least once a week), and in 1908 diversified into theatre with a season of Modest Mussorgsky's *Boris Godunov* at the Grand Opera. It proved successful enough for him to attempt a combined season of opera and the cheaper alternative of ballet the following year.

SAISON RUSSE

Saison Russe opened on 19 May 1909 with twelve performances at the Theatre du Chatelet. It was a richly diverse programme, including the operas *Prince Igor* and *Ivan the Terrible* by Rimsky-Korsakov, *Judith* by Serov and the prologue from Glinka's *Ruslan and Lyudmila*. Diaghilev was also introducing Russian ballet to the West, and the repertoire was equally exciting, with the Western premieres of Fokine's ballets *Le Pavillon d'Armide* and the Egyptian-themed *Cléopâtre* set to a compilation of music from Rimsky-Korsakov, Glinka, Moussorgsky and Glazunov plus the more traditional *Les Sylphides* and an innovative grouping of Russian dances under the collective title *Le Festin*.

Diaghilev had been lucky enough to engage the forceful Cecchetti as ballet master to forge a company style through his daily classes and to perform some of the character roles.

Through his connection with Gabriel Astruc, Diaghilev was funded by Baron de Rothschild and other major Parisian financiers; society women such as Misia Edwards (later Misia Sert), who became one of his most supportive patrons and friends; American-born Princess de Polignac (daughter of Isaac Singer, inventor of the sewing machine); and Countess Greffuhle (the great beauty who Marcel Proust immortalised in his masterpiece *A la recherché du temps perdu)*.

The Theatre du Chatelet was not a fashionable theatre and was a poor substitute for the Paris Opera, where Diaghilev had presented his concert season the previous year. Undeterred, Diaghilev collaborated with Gabriel Astruc to produce the most glamorous event on the social calendar. He spent a fortune filling the theatre with flowers and packing it with the crème de la crème of Paris society. To set the scene, he specified that beautiful young unaccompanied women be invited to sit in the front rows of the stalls. Diaghilev's entrepreneurial flair paid off. *Le tout-Paris* responded in force and the theatre was a sea of sables and diamonds: aristocrats, intellectuals, the avant-garde, critics, impresarios and artists, resplendent in full Parisian glamour and sense of occasion.

Diaghilev was confident of the quality of the company they were about to see – studded with the talent of many of the stars of the Imperial Theatre – but he visualised Nijinsky as its crown jewel, intrinsic to his plans. Although the original poster promoting the season featured Pavlova, Diaghilev had changed the focus to Nijinsky. He billed him as the new God of the Dance", following in the footsteps of the famous French dancer, Auguste Vestris – the toast of Paris a century earlier, the last male star of dance and the teacher of Marius Petipa and Auguste Bournonville (who took his teachings to Russia and Denmark, respectively).

As Diaghilev had hoped, the audience was transfixed from the moment Nijinsky leapt onto the stage. The classical purity of his dancing surpassed anything they had seen, and they immediately declared him beyond comparison with Vestris.

Nijinsky's charisma and virtuosity as the White Slave in *Le Pavillon d'Armide* proved a sensation. His exotic appearance in Bakst's first designs to be seen in the West – white tights; a gorgeous silk embroidered jacket; feathered turban and jewelled choker – together with the intensity of his stage presence and thrilling technique were a revelation to the Paris audience. They realised they were in the presence of a genius. Nijinsky became an overnight wonder; and his partner, Karsavina, was catapulted to stardom by her dazzling performance in *L'Oiseau de feu* (a reverse version of Petipa's Bluebird from *The Sleeping Beauty,* in which the woman is turned into the bird) in Bakst's fabulous costumes of flaming ostrich feathers with Nijinsky as her turbaned prince.

Adolf Bolm was another stunning success as the wild Tatar Chief of the "Polovtsian Dances" in *Prince Igor.*

During intervals, the audience bombarded the stage: it was so crowded that the dancers had to dodge about to prepare for the next acts. Karsavina had cut her leg on the bracelets of Nijinsky's costume for *Le Festin*. People were pointing at them and asking them questions. Reports of Nijinsky pacing up and down like a caged animal, fidgeting with his hands, indicate his inner turmoil.

The season was fuelled with a high sense of excitement: *Le tout-Paris* was rushing to view the exotic Saison Russe and its star. Fokine had choreographed his new ballets – *Le Pavillon d'Armide;* and *Cléopâtre,* specifically to display Nijinsky's talent. The Paris audiences raved that Nijinsky seemed to belong to another world: that he soared like a bird – that his leaps hovered midair. People swore that he stopped up there: he had a facility to stay still before his descent and his feet hardly appeared to touch the stage. For his exit at the end of a *pas de trois* with Karsavina and Alexandra Baldina in *Le Pavillon d'Armide,* Nijinsky spontaneously jumped off stage and "brought the house down" in applause. In Karsavina's words, "No-one in the audience could see him land; to all eyes, he floated up and vanished. A storm of applause broke: the orchestra had to stop."

In the interval, one of the stage invaders asked him how he did it. "You just have to stay up there a while," he said.

It was a technique mastered in the 20th century by Mikhail Baryshnikov – the later star of the Mariinsky stage, who has been frequently cited as a perpetuator of the Nijinsky legend. In the 1970s, Romola Nijinsky referred to Baryshnikov as her "adopted son" – "The first dancer in fifty years who resembles Vaslav in art, in technique and in his flying leaps." She did her best to enlist him to perpetuate the Nijinsky legend.

In *Cléopâtre,* Nijinsky was another slave – "Crouching low as a black panther at the feet of his Cleopatra [actress Ida Rubenstein]," wrote Bronislava, "in a display of erotic bestiality and mimicry which drove the audiences wild." Nijinsky caused a similar sensation in *Les Sylphides*, a ballet well known to the Paris audience but transformed by Nijinsky's thrilling technique and intense expression. It was a ballet in which Nijinsky could best demonstrate his interpretative powers – his ability to express an elusive poetic idea and to convey the essence of the music. The audience reported that the ethereal quality of the dancers touched their souls: their reaction rose ecstatically towards frenzy at the finale and they went wild, screaming and cheering.

Audiences were awed by Nijinsky's versatility as they watched his transformation from the ethereal weightless being of *Les Sylphides* to the sensuous slave of *Pavillon d'Armide* and spirited captain of the Lezgins – a wild mountain tribe from the remote high Caucasus – dancing the Georgian national *Lezginka* in the finale of *Le Festin*. Nijinsky thrived on the charged atmosphere on stage and the excited reaction of the audience. At the curtain calls, he reverted to his own personality, modestly stepping to the front of the stage, placing his right hand on his left shoulder and calmly sweeping his arm down in a flowing gesture with a composed inclination of his head.

The season moved at a demanding pace – between acts, Nijinsky needed time to prepare himself psychologically for his next role and recoiled from the trail of celebrities Diaghilev brought to his dressing room. Diaghilev treated the room as a salon, ignoring the fact that Nijinsky needed time alone between performances. The constantly crowded room must have been a strain on his psyche.

Nijinsky's dancing touched something in people: it reached beyond the traditional confines of the elite to the man on the street and drew the first truly appreciative, public audience to ballet. Through his artistic achievement in classical ballets such as *Les Sylphides*, Nijinsky showed how the *premier danseur* could be more than just a partner of the ballerina. He was not always the *premier danseur* or Prince – he was more often a puppet, a clown or a slave, but by his artistry at every level, Nijinsky's success elevated the art form of ballet and re-established its status in Western Europe.

It also created a new image for the male dancer. It gave birth to a new group of ballets choreographed as showcases for their skills – Fokine's ballets *Le Spectre de la rose, Petrushka, Narcisse* and *Le Dieu bleu* all created as vehicles for Nijinsky's talent.

Contrary to most people's beliefs, the Ballets Russes exuded a strong heterosexual image of virility and power. The dancers were strong and athletic – the men masculine, the women glamorous. All imbued the art form with a passion unseen before in Paris – a wild spontaneity that could have stemmed from the Russian Steppes. Much of Nijinsky's fascination was his androgyny, his strange mixture of delicacy and power. It was compellingly erotic.

The season was a turning point in many lives. On the personal level, Diaghilev's former lover and secretary, Alexis Mavrine, had left his master's way clear to focus on his new love, Nijinsky, by running off with one of the dancers, Olga Feodorovna – said to be the only woman who had ever attracted Diaghilev, the day after the Paris premiere. The new star was now frequently seen at Diaghilev's side – a silent presence at the late-night suppers Diaghilev attended with the avant-garde.

Saison Russe was a triumph – Diaghilev had found his true vocation, and Nijinsky's career was launched in the West. Diaghilev had set his sights on making his protégé the sensation of Paris – and later to conquer the world. Ballet was brought back into vogue in the West, escalating to heights previously unknown – the ballets were the drawcard of the season, not the operas. Despite the high quality of the opera performances, even *Prince Igor* was only remembered for the "Polovtsian Dances" that Fokine had choreographed and in which Adolf Bolm stirred the senses of the audience as the wild Warrior King, whereas Nijinsky was the talk of the town for his performances in the two Fokine ballets *Le Pavillon d'Armide* and *Cléopâtre,* the *divertissements* of *Le Festin* and *Les Sylphides,* which he danced with three ballerinas – Karsavina, Baldina and Pavlova.

Bronislava Nijinsky described the Saison Russe in her memoirs as an artistic milestone:

> *We felt that the spectators had witnessed the birth of a living art. For we artists had ourselves experienced something great being born in us. We felt as though we*

> *were walking in the clouds and this feeling of unreality stayed with us through the entire season.*

They were heady times: the dawn of a glorious new epoch in Western culture, now realised as the most significant period since the Renaissance. Apart from *Les Sylphides,* everything in the season was being seen for the first time outside Russia, including Mussorgsky's *Boris Godunov* – which today symbolises Russian opera. Diaghilev almost single-handedly introduced Russian art to the West, although he later moved on to create new works by European artists.

Diaghilev's chief interest was in new aesthetics – he was devoted to creating new works of art. To him, repetition was death. His talent for developing the arts was based on his latterly developed personal taste, his eye and ear for bringing creative people together. He brought artists to theatre design and commissioned new music and choreography. And he had no compunction in plundering existing work – rearranging it or adding in the works of other composers to create a new score, give it a new libretto, more dramatic impact, different choreography or fresh design. He took huge artistic risks in presenting the avant-garde. One of the best examples was *La Belle au bois dormant (The Sleeping Princess,* now *The Sleeping Beauty),* a Petipa ballet that was given the Diaghilev treatment much later in the history of the Ballets Russes (1921). As the company had no resident choreographer at the time, it was Diaghilev's creative solution to maintaining his commitment to present new works, and at the same time, present an example of the grand era of the Imperial Ballet. He commissioned Bakst to design five sets and about a hundred costumes. He replaced much of Tchaikovsky's score with music from his other compositions and commissioned Stravinsky to reorchestrate the prelude and Aurora's variation in Act 3. He engaged a former *regisseur* of the Mariinsky, Nicolas Sergeev, to recreate the choreography, directed much of it himself and invited Bronislava Nijinsky to choreograph fresh sequences such as the now-popular Three Ivans. Despite it all, the ballet was not an initial success. It was several years before the company could reclaim the sets and costumes from the London presenter who had confiscated them in lieu of box office takings.

Nevertheless, the following year, when he needed to mount a new work in a hurry for the Paris season, Diaghilev had the idea of extracting some of the best dances from *The Sleeping Princess* and presenting them as a *divertissement*. To cut costs, he resurrected the sets of *Le Pavillon d'Armide*. So was born the spectacle of *Aurora's Wedding* – a classic one-act ballet, still regularly performed by major companies and reverently reproduced precisely as Diaghilev mixed and matched it at the time.

As an impresario, Diaghilev took constant risks in continuously commissioning new works and never sacrificing quality to cost. Few arts companies would take such risks today.

The risks he took in 1909 were underwritten by his confidence in Nijinsky.

Despite his introspective personality, Nijinsky was not overly affected by the adulation he received as the new wonder of the Western world. It was no new phenomenon to him after winning over the exacting St Petersburg audiences. Although it was not something he sought, he had learnt to accept being paid attention to and discussed in detail, since entering the Imperial School at the age of nine. But Paris was a highly sophisticated city, and he was being feted at the highest level. His circle of fanatical worshippers was growing wider by the night. Nijinsky's reaction was to withdraw more into himself. He dutifully accompanied Diaghilev on his social rounds but paid less than lip service to the public, preferring to focus on his dancing life.

INTERPRETER

Nijinsky practised long hours each day and continuously worked on his technique, but I am told by his family, Tamara and Kinga – and reflected in the writings of Romola and Bronislava – that his genius verged on the supernatural. His supreme skill as a performer was his mysterious ability to transform himself to fit each role. His perfect technique and personality disappeared into the character he was portraying. Nijinsky the dancer disappeared into a soulful Albrecht mourning the untimely death of Giselle or a sensuous slave tending his mistress Armida's whims in *Le Pavillon d'Armide*.

From his early days, Nijinsky was most drawn to roles he could personally create or reinterpret. Choreography was much looser in those days – it served only as a theme, and dancers had the freedom to work on the details of their own roles if they felt inclined. Nijinsky always worked on his solos and improvisation, such as the Bluebird *divertissement* of Petipa's *The Sleeping Beauty*, when he was at the Imperial School. He dramatically altered the movement, rhythm and expression and revised the make-up and costume to create a completely new interpretation. He persuaded the wardrobe department to discard the existing cumbersome costume they had inherited from the court ballets of Louis XI of a full-skirted coat and skirt with restricting curved wings covering the arms and hands, which restricted movement. Nijinsky customised a simple tunic and shorts over tights and lighter wings. The new costume freed his movements in performance and pleased the St Petersburg crowds of normally conservative balletomanes. Nijinsky's sister, Bronislava, writes of her impression in her memoirs: "The body of Nijinsky seemed to lose its human contours and become a bird in flight."

Such a feat is incomprehensible to us in the identity-driven arena of the 21st century, where watching stars such as Rudolf Nureyev and Mikhail Baryshnikov performing a role is just that. It is beyond the imagination to forget who they are, no matter what costume they wear or how brilliant their performance is. Given his extraordinary stage presence, it is little wonder that Nijinsky is still referred to as the God of the Dance. Technique has developed in such leaps and bounds over the last century that Nijinsky's feats of 1909 would be tame to audiences today, but his stage presence – an indefinable quality beyond technique – would have set him apart any age.

Nijinsky clearly had that rare "star quality" that transports a performance beyond the steps – he "lived the dance".

It was partly due to his intuitive understanding of meditation. His metamorphosis on stage appeared to be the result of self-transformation – of entering a meditative spiritual state – a trance, which moved him beyond consciousness of technique. It was not something he ever discussed, but he was observed preparing for it at the side of the stage.

It was this connection with his inner self that made Nijinsky's difference – a major key to why he is still revered. He had realised as a child that he did not easily relate to people and as a teenager at boarding school had become accustomed to solitude. He later wrote in his notebooks, which gained fame as *The Diary of Vaslav Nijinsky*: "I like to hide myself from people and am therefore used to living alone." He was not well equipped with verbal skills. The stage was the outlet for his energy, expression and his escape into an imaginary world. The only mention he made was a reference in the diary he wrote: "I am a man in a trance … I can write in a trance … I am in a trance of God."

This self-sufficiency is the probable cause of his mystique – the elusive "secret" that set him apart.

Bronislava was one of the first people determined to discover this secret.

> *I wanted to understand the fascination Nijinsky exerted on the public, a fascination that so captured the imagination, there were those who claimed that in his dance Nijinsky's feet never touched the ground. I wanted to understand those qualities of his dance that I felt depended not so much on his huge leaps, his extraordinary elevation or the amazing virtuosity of his dance technique, but rather the nature of the Dance, living in him, body and soul.*
>
> *He prepared as if in meditation, gathering within himself an inner soul force that he could carry onto the stage and offer to the audience.*

It was Nijinsky's creative visualisation that gave his characters the edge: he had instinctively perfected the technique before anyone coined the word. Benois informs us:

> *Having put on the costume, he gradually began to change into another being – the one he saw in the mirror. He became reincarnated and actually entered into his new existence, as an exceptionally attractive and poetic personality.*

The British critic, bookseller Cyril Beaumont, who faithfully documented the London history of Diaghilev's Ballets Russes, described Nijinsky's skill as "Dr Jekyll with more than one Mr Hyde".

It is possible that Nijinsky was able to achieve his transformation because of his simple ego – because he was a natural artist, he had no empty vanity. In his diary, Nijinsky emphasises feeling – that is, emotion mixed with instinct, differentiating between "feeling" people and others, saying, "People must do as they feel."

At the time of his takeover of the Paris public, one of the many people on whom Nijinsky made a lasting impression was Boris Kochno, later Diaghilev's secretary, close friend, librettist, and preferred successor at the Ballets Russes. He wrote:

> *One had the impression of an unreal, weightless being, a spirit.... Watching Nijinsky move, one could not believe he was subject to the law of gravity, nor think that his breathing had to be rigidly controlled, that his movements required great effort... the first appearance of Nijinsky on the Paris stage lives in my memory as a visitation of absolute beauty.*

French poet-playwright, impresario, filmmaker (*Beauty and the Beast*) and society cynic, Jean Cocteau, was besotted by Nijinsky's genius. The thin, fashionably dressed man, often wearing rouge and lipstick, was almost always hanging around Nijinsky and drooling about him in print. Cocteau was a leading member of the Diaghilev circus who drew many of the historical caricatures, including the poster of *Le Spectre de la rose* used for the first Ballets Russes season, and wrote the libretto for one of Nijinsky's most sublime characters, the Blue God (in *Le Dieu bleu*).

PERSON

The adulation and accolades, effusive and descriptive accounts of Nijinsky's dancing are endless. Nobody who saw him perform ever forgot the experience, but what of the man himself? He was living his art on stage away from the constraints of the imperial regime, he was admired and accepted more than ever before, he was surrounded by those he loved – his mother had come to Paris to see him and Bronislava perform – he was growing closer to Diaghilev. However, it was not without personal cost: he was on the brink of dominance by Diaghilev, to the detriment of his own needs and way of life. He was a very private person, dependent on his own space, and he resented the constant crowds in Diaghilev's wake. Onstage, he spiralled away from the demands of Diaghilev's flamboyant world into his multidimensional other lives.

Offstage, Nijinsky was another being: to the Paris intelligentsia, he appeared unintelligent and ordinary – almost sexless to the public eye and impossible to know as a person. He made no contact with the other dancers – he hardly ever spoke to them and only walked about picking his fingers, looking at them for a long time and then walking away. A century later, he remains an enigma – he lived so intensely inside himself that his personal identity was unclear. People took great pains to meet him to boost their own sense of celebrity. It was no easy feat – because of Nijinsky's own need for privacy and his lover's proprietary guarding, he was only accessible through Diaghilev. Anyone who did manage to meet him was inevitably disappointed. It was frustratingly difficult to relate the detached, unremarkable-looking foreigner to the magical performer on stage.

Nijinsky offered them nothing of himself. Because he appeared to be inarticulate and had little command of French, people spoke to him as if he were a child. He had no concept of social conversation or diplomacy and was a misfit in the profile of the glamorous company. In Diaghilev's cultured circle, he remained on the periphery and rarely contributed to the conversation. In his own mind, he had come to the conclusion that it was better to be silent than talk nonsense, although he was avidly listening and absorbing anything he perceived to be of benefit. He was almost an invisible member of the group, obvious mostly for his nervous habits of picking his fingers and pacing around. He was remote from the other dancers and acted as if he or they were aliens. It was as if Nijinsky existed only through dancing. Offstage, he was a shadow, onstage, a star.

SECOND SIGHT

My conversations with Nijinsky's grandchildren included discussions of spirituality.

Kinga's husband John presented me with a book about second sight.

During our conversations in Phoenix, I ask several times about the family in Europe. They're all mad, I am dismissively told.

Several years later, after putting Nijinsky aside, I decided to contact Nijinsky's grandson – his elder daughter Kyra's son Vaslav Markevitch in Italy. He had been living in Switzerland for many years working for the Red Cross but recently moved to a small village in Tuscany. Our introduction is brokered by Christopher Lyndon Jones, who was writing a biography of Vaslav's famous musician father, Igor Markevitch. He encouraged me in my quest to the degree of telling me a good place to stay in Florence. Markevitch responds to my tentative approach with warmth and friendliness. He apologises for not inviting me to stay, as his furniture has not arrived, but suggests a hotel in the nearby village of Acquaviva.

I am a little confused that he calls himself Marco Vinci, but he explains that he was brought up by friends of his stepmother in Italy, where he is known by that name.

The heat is almost unbearable, and the trains are all delayed at Florence Station. The second-class carriage of the train to Naples is crowded and dirty. I manage to get off at a place called Chiusi and recognise Vaslav immediately. He has a small goatee beard, dark hair (dyed), dark skin, strong features, glasses, a guttural voice and is walking with the support of two sticks because, he tells me, he recently broke his hip in Spain. He is younger and less formal than I expected and comes across as a quaint combination of proper English/European gentleman and eccentric Bohemian/ Russian count. His conversation is very bright and sharp and his personality overwhelming. I can hardly get a word in edgeways and can see how has worn out his wives. Vaslav/Marco drives me to my hotel, Tiziana, in the little village of Acquaviva. No-one speaks English, and Vaslav takes over my check-in.

The hotel is crowded with large parties of farmers, so we drive up to a hilltop trattoria with starched tablecloths and passable food.

During the conversation, Vaslav tells me that he has found the secret to climate control (in 2005) and has a couple of governments interested, but they are hesitant to accept his theories because of his lack of university degrees. He is a disciple of the late volcanologist Jacques Cousteau.

Later in the conversation, he tells me he is an ET – an extra-terrestrial being – and is tired because he was woken in the night by messages, which often take hours to transcribe. "How do you receive them?" I ask.

"Through the numbers on my watch," he replies.

He drives me back to my hotel in the village, arranging to collect me in the morning to continue the interview.

The next day, the conversation takes a bizarre turn when Vaslav tells me that his grandmother Romola told him on her deathbed that Tamara was not Nijinsky's daughter. He embellishes his story with details off the record.

Vaslav suddenly spirals the interview further downwards by telling me he had thought I could be his next wife. He then accuses me of exploiting the Nijinsky name. I am trapped in his garden in a surreal situation with no phone or means of escape.

Eventually, he drives me back to the village.

I catch the train back to Florence in shock, pondering the revelations and the Nijinsky family's relationship with the supernatural. During my sojourn with the other Nijinskys in Phoenix, Kinga talked several times of Nijinsky's connection to the supernatural world. She also gave me a couple of books to read on "second sight." In *The Eagle and the Rose,* the medium writes of her spirit guide communicating through certain signs and symbols – a "language of its own, foreign to most people – complex and totally unexplainable."

Perhaps Nijinsky's family are attempting to access the key to their illustrious ancestor's inner life.

MENTOR

Unlike his grandson, Nijinsky's thoughts were not apparent until the advent of his choreography – which many people doubted at the time to be his own concepts. It was assumed that he was heavily influenced in his life and work by Diaghilev. It was a reasonable assumption – Diaghilev was incapable of loving anyone without trying to educate them and bring out their latent qualities. He showed love by teaching. Diaghilev protected Nijinsky from the outside world and gave him artistic freedom in the Ballet Russes that he would never have had in Russia. He also influenced Nijinsky's development as an artist, educating him culturally by taking him to galleries and concerts and exposing him to avant-garde artists and intellectuals. Nijinsky writes in his diary: "Diaghilev did not like me because I composed ballets myself ... Diaghilev liked showing that Nijinsky was his pupil in everything." Diaghilev was a true trailblazer, but he was breaking new ground in an area in which he was not very experienced and needed Nijinsky's genius to reflect his own glory. But the resulting cost to Nijinsky was the loss of his independence and inner freedom. Nijinsky's sister Bronislava noticed how her brother changed his personality, becoming more withdrawn and showing signs of repression, after meeting Diaghilev.

At the end of the season, Nijinsky became very ill with typhoid, caused by drinking water straight from the tap after a performance and possibly exacerbated by the stresses of the season. It was luckily not a severe case, but he was confined to bed for a month. Diaghilev saw to it that he was well tended to by a doctor who treated the imperial family but kept outside the door of his room for fear of illness himself. Diaghilev was both superstitious and a hypochondriac. He reacted alarmingly to any signs of "misfortune", such as a black cat in the theatre, and refused to travel by sea as a gypsy had once told him he would die on the water. Although a risk-taker in his work, he took no physical risks in his person. It was during this period that Diaghilev made Nijinsky an offer that he "couldn't refuse", partly for economic reasons – he had incurred serious debt through the season. Diaghilev offered to personally support Nijinsky if he lived with him full-time. He would no longer be under contract and on salary, but all his living expenses would be paid, and his mother would receive an allowance in St Petersburg.

According to Nijinsky, Diaghilev realised his value and was afraid he might leave him "because I wanted to leave even then, when I was twenty years old". Writing in his diary, in a later state of unbalance, Nijinsky purports that he was persuaded by Diaghilev, because "I was afraid of life. I did not know that I was God".

RETURN TO RUSSIA

It was an anticlimax for the group to return to the conservatism of St Petersburg after the heady excitement of Paris. The Imperial Theatre and Diaghilev's improvised company were different worlds. Diaghilev had offered them an irresistible opportunity with his ability to generate ideas and develop artists.

When Nijinsky arrived back after his convalescence, the *St Petersburg Gazette* reported that he appeared untouched by his great success:

> *Dressed modestly, shy, with a very boyish appearance, Nijinsky does not look like the hero of the brilliant Russian season in Paris, which scored such success in that contemporary Babylon. He speaks just like a child. He gets worked up and blushes just as if he is embarrassed by his celebrity.*

As a consequence of his success outside their domain, and with the officially out-of-favour Diaghilev, Nijinsky was punished by the Imperial Theatre. He was fined for minor offences such as lateness for class and cast in lesser roles. As a result, his performances lacked the dynamism of the stimulating Diaghilev stage.

SECOND SAISON RUSSE

On the strength of his artistic success – although not at the box office – Diaghilev was already planning a second season of ballet in Paris for the following year. With the help of Gabriel Astruc, a new supporter, Baron Dimitri de Gunzburg – who paid his considerable outstanding debts from the previous season – and a newly acquired wealthy patron, Misia Edwards (who later married Spanish painter Jose-Maria Sert), Diaghilev was eventually able to muster enough support to arrange another season in 1910. Diaghilev's life was always dictated by patronage, never by budgets, for which he had an eye as astute as his artistic judgment.

The second season was presented at the Grand Paris Opera with two new programmes carefully selected to build on the interest Diaghilev had regenerated in the art form of ballet by offering yet more titillation of the senses in newer, splashier stagings of the classics and new works packed with new artistic ideas – choreographically, musically and in design terms.

After the sensation of 1909, the aristocratic and literary circles at the Café de la Paix, which Diaghilev frequented in Paris, were in a twitter of anticipation. Theatregoers won over by the glamour and spectacle of the entrepreneurial Diaghilev troupe the year before were looking for further excitement.

They were not disappointed: the first programme of the second season in 1910 consisted of *Carnaval,* the premiere of *Scheherazade,* another variation of the successful compilation idea of *Le Festin* and the Romantic classic *Giselle.*

Carnaval was an instant success when Fokine adapted the "Harlequinade" *divertissement* he had created earlier as entertainment for a ball in St Petersburg. The familiar figures of the commedia dell'arte – Harlequin, Columbine, Pierrot and Pantaloon – had spilled down from the stage to flit amongst the guests in an atmosphere of frivolity. It was a perfect party ballet. Fokine restaged it for the Ballets Russes, and it premiered at the Theater des Westens in Charlottenburg, Berlin, en route to Paris.

Carnaval proved a great success as the opening ballet of the 1910 season – Nijinsky was much admired in the role of Harlequin, dressed in a thin tight-fitting costume and tights, which would have seriously shocked the conservative regime in St Petersburg. According to Bronislava, "It revealed each muscle – which vibrated with joy." His dazzling display of bravura was applauded by audience and critic alike and the role was pronounced one of his greatest achievements.

Nijinsky's Harlequin greatly appealed to Cocteau, who described it as:

> *An acrobatic cat stuffed with full of candid lechery and crafty indifference, a schoolboy, wheedling, thieving, swift-footed, utterly freed of the chains of gravity, a creature of perfect mathematical grace. Desire, mischief, self-satisfaction, arrogance, rapid bobbings of the head... and specially a way of peering out from under the visor of the cap he wore pulled down over his eyebrows, the way one shoulder was raised higher than the other and his cheek pressed against it, the way the right hand was outstretched, the leg poised to relax, such (and it was something never before granted me to see or hear in the theatre) was Vaslav Nijinsky in Carnaval, surrounded by an uninterrupted roar of applause.*

When the ballet was seen in London in 1911, the prominent ballet critic Beaumont was equally impressed:

> *Think of him one moment poised in an attitude of mockery, the next bounding and rebounding in the air with the ease of a bouncing rubber ball, or twirling around with the facility and precision of a spun wheel. All his movements were precisely timed; the gracefully extended hand with the beckoning finger; the impish mockery of his one big step to Columbine's dainty two, as they entered with their arms around each other's waists; then his thrilling solo with the pirouette a la grande seconde, ending in his unflurried sitting on the ground with crossed legs. He did not so much as dance to the music, he appeared to issue from it. His dancing was music made visible.*

The second ballet on the 1910 Paris programme was *Scheherazade.* It was the hit of the season, tapping the fascination of the time for the East with such outstanding success that it became the early image of the Ballet Russes. The ballet epitomised all the excitement that the exotic Eastern company brought to the jaded Parisian palate. A fantasy dance drama based on a story from the Arabian Nights, *Scheherazade* was ribald with burning passion and barbaric colour. Its lush décor and sensual theme set the trend for exotica and things oriental around the world for years to come. Its radical colour combination of green and blue was copied immediately by the high fashion jewellery house of Cartier and the original designs of Bakst's exotic sets and costumes were bought by the Musee des Arts Decoratifs. Like almost everything about *Scheherazade,* they have become much-copied classics.

The ballet also set the fashion choreographically. Nijinsky dazzled audiences as the Golden Slave: he was the talk of the town for his bestiality. Clad in gold brocade trousers and turban, flashing jewellery and gold bracelets, his body painted a bizarre blue-grey hue, Nijinsky shimmied around the stage – half snake, half panther, his performance climaxing in a death-frenzy pirouette on his head – a forerunner of the breakdancing of today.

Nijinsky is said to have choreographed his solo himself. Proust wrote that he had never seen anything so beautiful. Benois described Nijinsky as "half cat, half snake, fiendishly agile, feminine and yet wholly terrifying". Cocteau was even more carried away: "Nijinsky jumps like a young beast of prey that has been kept locked in darkness and is now intoxicated by the light." Nijinsky was the name on everybody's lips, and the fashion in everything was Ballets Russes.

The only blot on the success was a serious inaccuracy of credit: Benois, who devised the concept for the ballet and wrote the libretto, was shocked when he opened the programme to see that it had been attributed to Bakst. During the performance, he was buoyed up by *Scheherazade's* success, but the elation was soon eroded by the injustice of losing his rights. When he questioned Diaghilev, Benois was flippantly told that Bakst needed a ballet! Benois declared he had split from Diaghilev forever and left Paris. It was shabby, unethical treatment by Diaghilev of a key collaborator who had supported him since the days of *Mir Iskusstva.* Benois was one of the original members of the Pickwickians, an artist, scholar and historian who had been a major force behind Diaghilev's early projects and the real ballet-lover in the group who, after the Second World War, became the director of the Hermitage Museum in St Petersburg.

Giselle was a totally different matter. It was a ballet very familiar to the Paris audience, although it had not been seen there for forty years. Taking *Giselle* back to Paris was intended as a (backhanded – showing Diaghilev's superior presentation) compliment to the French, despite the high standard it imposed on the company, and a challenge for Diaghilev: presenting a ballet in its place of origin is a venture still practised by companies wanting to prove their standing in the 21st century.

It was the reason for Nijinsky worrying more about his role as Albrecht than any other. It was one of his few opportunities to express himself through pure dance, without masquerading as a slave or a clown. Nijinsky saw it as the ultimate classical role – the challenge of his career. He aimed to bare Albrecht's soul, to follow his emotional journey, and not just dance the steps or repeat the traditional gestures. In preparing to spiritually identify with the role, Nijinsky wrote reams of notes and rethought every dramatic move. His changes upset his partner Karsavina, whom he had not informed about his new ideas. She burst into tears in frustration when he did not respond to her acting during rehearsals, not realising that he was concentrating on trying to instinctively reinterpret his own role.

The ballet was a success, but not a sensation: having experienced the heady excitement of Diaghilev's novelties, the Paris audience was more interested in ballets depicting the exotic Russian character or anything new. Once again, Diaghilev's instincts proved right; he had been reluctant to programme a classic like *Giselle* for that reason and was only persuaded by the quality of his stars and their new presentation.

Like all his roles, Nijinsky's interpretation of Albrecht offered something original: he gave the role an emotional identity that changed the focus of the ballet from the sole plight of the peasant girl Giselle to include her Hamlet-like lover. The change of emphasis greatly impressed the new Director of the Imperial Theatres, Vladimir Telyakovsky (he had replaced Volkonsky, who resigned after Diaghilev's dismissal), who was on a visit to Paris to observe Diaghilev's venture. He proffered the previously missing Imperial Theatres endorsement by announcing that he would be including *Giselle* in the next Mariinsky season with Anna Pavlova and Vaslav Nijinsky in the leading roles.

The second of the two 1910 programmes consisted of *Les Sylphides, Les Orientales,* two solo *divertissements* – "Danse Siamoise" and "Kobold" – for Nijinsky and a new ballet, *L'Oiseau de feu* (not to be confused with the Bluebird *pas de deux* from *The Sleeping Beauty,* performed under that name in the previous season), which was set to music by Diaghilev's latest discovery, Igor Stravinsky. *L'Oiseau de feu* was intended for Pavlova, but instead shot Karsavina, partnered by Fokine, to eternal fame for her electrifying performance – as it did Margot Fonteyn forty-six years later in a reconstruction by Grigoriev for the Royal Ballet to celebrate the 25th anniversary of Diaghilev's death.

“Danse Siamoise” was a quasi-Oriental solo inspired by a visit to St Petersburg of the Siamese Court Dancers, which Fokine had cleverly recalled from some years back.

“Kobold” was another solo to a piano composition by Greig, orchestrated by Stravinsky, which Nijinsky choreographed himself.

SUMMONS

The success of his first two seasons promoted Diaghilev to seriously consider forming a permanent company. Meanwhile, Nijinsky was faced with another issue that was to plague his next few years: he received a summons for military service. This time, he was granted a reprieve as he was recovering from typhoid, but it was not as easily resolved in the coming years.

Following the success of his Albrecht in Paris, Nijinsky gave another stunning performance back at the Mariinsky in St Petersburg. It is unlikely that he was surprised by a call to the office of the Assistant Director of the Imperial Theatres the next morning: his promotion from soloist to principal artist was long overdue and it was natural to assume that his performance of the night before had brought about that recognition. He was one of the leading dancers of the company and had been performing principal roles since the beginning of his contract three years before.

It was a tremendous shock to his family when Nijinsky returned from the meeting with the news that he had been dismissed from the Imperial Theatre. He had been told that the reason for his dismissal was his disobedience in wearing an indecent costume in Act 1 of *Giselle* in the presence of Empress Dowager Cixi. It was the same costume he had worn in Paris but did differ from the conventional Imperial Theatre wear. Bakst had designed a simpler, more practical style for the Paris season that was less cumbersome and showed a better bodyline – the "line" dancers always strive to achieve. Bakst had shortened the jacket of the costume and discarded the shorts, which were traditionally worn over the tights.

The unheralded introduction of the era of the tights in Russia was a shock to the conservative hierarchy and audience. By today's terms, the Albrecht costume was innocuous, but tights without covering shorts were considered offensive in an age when any public hint of homosexuality was condemned – irrespective of what went on in private.

The *St Petersburg Gazette* described Nijinsky's costume and noted that the women in the audience appeared quite satisfied with it, deliberately looking at it through their lorgnettes.

It turned out to be their only opportunity, as Nijinsky was fired before the next performance of the ballet and replaced by another dancer – Samuel Andrianov – wearing the traditional gear.

The dismissal was drastic: there is still a question mark about why such a serious action was taken against one of the Mariinsky's major artists. It would appear that there was much unstated at the time, and a plethora of theories still shroud the truth. The rigidity of the Imperial Theatre regime caused it to be riddled with political intrigue, but it is one of those ironies of fate that Nijinsky was not politically active, or even aware: he was one of the few people who remained oblivious of all undercurrents as he continued to focus on his dancing.

One of the theories surrounding the scandal is that the dismissal was a consequence of Nijinsky turning down the request to partner the politically powerful Kschessinska. Another theory is that Diaghilev engineered it by deliberately altering Nijinsky's costume, to free him full-time for the Ballets Russes. Yet another is that he was a scapegoat for Diaghilev: that it was the imperial court's way of getting back at Diaghilev to discredit his enterprises and associations because he had fallen out of favour – his unconventional ideas had ruffled a few feathers. It was later revealed that the empress knew nothing of what was happening and told a friend at court that she regretted Nijinsky's expulsion. Whatever the truth, it has remained a mystery, like so many facts surrounding this extraordinary artist.

There are differing accounts of the episode in the Nijinsky biographies: Romola wrote that Nijinsky failed to wear the traditional male dancer's undergarment (the jockstrap) and was told by Director Krupensky to change his costume before going on stage, but Nijinsky refused that, and a similar order from Telyakovsky. The mostly reliable Nijinsky biographer, Richard Buckle, suggests that there was no question of omitting the undergarment and that Nijinsky refused to change his costume when he was told to wear trunks over tights and that Telayakovsky was not in the theatre that night. Vera Krasovskaya quoted from Telyakovsky's diaries that the costume "produced a sensation not only in the public, but chiefly in the tsar's loge. Empress Maria Fedorovna sent Grand Duke Sergei Mikhailovich to find out what costume Nijinsky would wear in the next act, for if it was to be the same one, she and the Grand Duchesses intended to leave the theater".

Years later, in 1979, Roland John Wiley of the University of Michigan wrote in *The Dancing Times* of the furore in the press at the time, culminating in the publication of the complete exchange of views between Nijinsky and Telyakovsky in the most theatre-oriented of the newspapers, the *St Petersburg Gazette.* The first of Nijinsky's explanations of the events was introduced as:

> *An unheard of commotion in the ballet – there has never been anything in the annals of our Terpsichore like the dismissal of an artist from service in 24 hours! This is how the victim – Mr Nijinsky himself, explains the incident.*
>
> *"Having returned not long ago from abroad where I appeared in Paris, Brussels and Berlin, I diligently began to prepare myself for the season in the Imperial Mariinsky Theatre. After several postponements of my debut the directorate put Giselle into the repertoire with me in the leading male role.*
>
> *"Appearing for the first time before the Petersburg public in this ballet, I wanted to create the most favourable conditions for my debut, and for that reason requested permission*

from the manager of the office of the imperial theatres to appear in the costumes in which I appeared five times, and not without success, on the stage of the first theatre of the world – the Paris Grand Opera – in the Russian ballet performances ballet of last year. A(lexander) Ya(kovelich) Golovine kindly permitted me to carry out my intention.

"The costumes in question were executed exactly from drawings of the famous Russian artist and art critic Alexander Nikolaevich Benois.

"Never entering into any appraisal of the works of such masters as Benois, Bakst, Golovine, Korovine and others, and strictly subordinating myself to their artistic authority, I believed that, having worn the Parisian costumes and having brought them with me, I could only contribute to the artistic success of my first appearance.

"When indeed, being dressed, I was about to go onstage, into my dressing room came Mr Mettsner, the manager of the production department, and to my amazement declared that he found it impossible to admit me to the performance in this costume. Having conveyed this rather belated news to me Mr Mettsner hastened to leave the dressing room before I managed to respond to it.

"At that time expecting further instructions, I went on to the stage where I met the artist Golovine, who looked me over and declared to me 'out of friendship' that he feared my costume could displease because of the tricot which was raised too high. I got upset and asked: 'What am I to do?' But Golovine answered nothing to this and cut short the conversation. At this time AD Krupensky was on stage along with other persons from the directorate, but nobody said a word to me.

"In a few minutes I heard the first notes of the ballet, and in no event wanting to 'break off' the performance, and

on the other hand, having received no instructions, I went out to perform my role. The public's attitude toward my dances is well known to you.

"Behind the scenes, apart from what I told you, nothing more took place and all the talk, which is spreading around the city about me allegedly 'disobeying' is sheer ridiculous fabrication. I could not disobey anything for the simple reason that nobody ordered me to do anything. The next morning I was called to the directorate, and AD Krupensky announced to me that I was dismissed from service in the imperial theatres for the first of my costumes.

"Without entering into a discussion of this fact, I can only say that if the directorate of the imperial theatres wanted me to stay in service they had two very simple means – either insist that I exchange my costume for one belonging to the state or quickly transfer my role to another artist, to either Legat or Andrianov. Both of them were onstage at the time and furthermore have repeatedly performed my role in Giselle.

"But once the directorate found it possible nevertheless to let me go into the overflowing hall in my costume I think that any responsibility was removed from me for this fact, and why I am the sole victim of the blunders of others is completely incomprehensible to me.

"In any event, during my many years of study in the theatre school and the short three years of my service, I strained every effort not to discredit the dignity of the surroundings that fostered me, and to maintain to the extent of my powers, at first in Russia and then abroad, the prestige and fame of our choreographic art. I recompense for this the directorate released its student and employee in 24 hours – I would not fire my servant from my home for a much more serious offence than appearing in an unfortunate costume – dressed with the permission of the very same

directorate that had not given me instructions pertaining to this matter either before or during the performance.

"Leaving the Russian stage under such conditions and all the same rather prematurely, at twenty, I hope that I find a place somewhere where I will be evaluated and judged for my artistic ability and not on the basis of a dress or costume in which I will perchance be dressed.

"To you, perhaps, much in my account appears strange and unintelligible, but I assure you that it is also unintelligible to me, those official reasons which so quickly and so irrevocably 'tied up' my artistic work which in Russia had barely begun."

The same article had a quote from Benois:

I don't quite know what to say. In my view no costume can be either decent or indecent. The question of decency and indecency is a question resolved with difficulty. (Ida) Rubenstein, who appeared in Cléopâtre almost nude, was decent, and at the same time some half-revealing girl in Alcazar produces the opposite impression. When the wish is only to show the frame then it is indecent, but once the baring is made on agreement with the epoch one cannot speak of pornography.

The reviewer from *Discourse* argued:

One appearance of Nijinsky could itself provide, in the present repertoire, artistic interest enough for the current ballet season. In the Mariinsky Theatre there is, besides Nijinsky, not one strong artistic talent and Nijinsky's equal in magnitude does not in general exist on ballet stages. Nijinsky is frankly necessary for a theatre, which is seriously striving toward the uplifting and renewal of ballet.

One might think that there are dozens of Nijinsky's at the disposal of the directorate if it can, with such ease and extravagance, sacrifice a ballet artist unique in the world only because the jacket in which he performed Giselle turned out to be a few centimetres higher than the "established model".

It was a devastating blow to Nijinsky's mother, who had dreamed of a secure future for her son. It meant the loss of the protection of the tsar, permanent employment and a pension for life, plus the blocking of matters such as compulsory military service.

By 1910, Nijinsky was one of the most valued and highest-paid male dancers in the Mariinsky company – his salary had been raised to 960 rubles, despite his frequent absences with Diaghilev. It is inexplicable that the Imperial Theatre would want to let him go.

At the age of twenty-one, Nijinsky therefore threw his hat in with Diaghilev – another reject of imperial service. In actual fact, there were many positive aspects to the dismissal. Nijinsky's straightforward personality only allowed him allegiance to one cause or party at a time. To some degree, it must have been a relief to escape the stagnant environment of the Imperial Ballet. Performing life with Diaghilev was an exhilarating journey of discovery and Nijinsky's "expulsion" accelerated Diaghilev's plans for his permanent company. Bronislava Nijinsky immediately resigned in support of her brother; followed by many of the other Imperial Theatre artists, including Tamara Karsavina and Ludmilla Schollar – both of whom were regular partners of Nijinsky – and Adolf Bolm.

BALLETS RUSSES 1911

Unbeknown to him, Nijinsky had performed for the last time on the Russian stage. It was also the last time he saw his beloved country of birth. Putting aside the drama of his changed circumstances, he headed expectantly to Monte Carlo for the opening of the first season of the Ballets Russes on 9 April 1911. Nijinsky was the pièce de résistance of a new ballet – *Le Spectre de la rose.*

Really just a male solo (although a work for two performers), *Le Spectre de la rose* was to become one of his most famous roles. Fokine had created the ballet in just a few days after being reminded of an idea suggested by a ballet critic while he was watching the scene in *Carnaval* in which Chiarina throws a rose to Eusebius.

Based on a poem by Théophile Gautier, set to the music of Carl Maria von Weber's *Invitation to the Dance,* the story is the reversal of the story of *La Sylphide*. It is a "romantic" dream come to life: a girl who has just returned from a ball dreams that she is visited by the spirit of the rose she had carried. It was one of Fokine's finest creations, lifted from a simple *pas de deux* (duet) by the partnership of Nijinsky and Karsavina to an experience never forgotten by those who saw it. One critic remarked that it is not often that two people fit their parts as Nijinsky and Karsavina in *Spectre.*

Nijinsky was at the height of his genius. His final leap offstage through the bedroom window became the famous symbol of his great elevation. It is still his best-remembered feat. Although the window was only about three or four inches high, the strength and length of the leap – the climax of a long variation – was so forceful that Nijinsky had to either be caught in his valet's arms offstage or land on a mattress. The ovation that invariably followed usually drowned out the orchestra. The apocryphal story is that Nijinsky's leap in *Spectre* beat the world long jump record of the time.

The former artistic director of the Australian Ballet, David McAllister, who performed Nijinsky's role in *Spectre* for Paul Cox's film of 2001, is quoted as having modestly said that he found the historic challenge so daunting that he hoped cinematic tricks would help the famous leap out of the window live up to its legend.

Nijinsky's airy lightness and ability to look as if he was flying through the air without touching the ground gave an illusion of an inhuman being. No other dancer has achieved the same effect: he appeared to be the very spirit of the rose, not a man in rose petals pretending to be a flower. It was the epitome of his androgyny: only an artist of Nijinsky's natural assurance could have carried off an appearance in Bakst's very feminine costume of rose petals, which were individually pinned on the costume he was sewn into each night. The Ballets Russes moved on to Paris, opening at Theatre du Chatelet on 6 June 1911 with a programme of *Carnaval* and the new ballets *Narcisse, Le Spectre de la rose* and *Sadko*. The second programme included *Scheherazade* and *Carnaval* and the premiere of *Petrushka* – all ballets that displayed Nijinsky's full talent and were his most renowned roles. Nijinsky's immersion in each role and intuitive artistry enabled him to create deep and complete dramatic images, which often initially camouflaged weaknesses in Fokine's choreography – with such a rush of artistic output, it was often sketchy and unfinished.

Narcissus was hastily created as Nijinsky's main role in the next programme when *Daphnis et Chloé* had to be postponed because Ravel had not completed the score. It must have been frustrating for Fokine, who was passionate about the concept and had been working on the choreography for several years. He was pressured into creating *Narcisse* as a substitute. It was not a recipe for success – Tcherepnin's lack of time was reflected in the score and the weak, uninspired choreography. The story was based on the Greek myth of Narcissus and his Echo (danced by Karsavina). Nijinsky's crash-landing entrance on stage was choreographically strained and awkward, killing any illusion of godlike flying. And there was a plethora of posturing. The ballet was carried by the quality of Nijinsky's dancing (helped by the fact that he was trying out a new technique for his own choreography, which rejected the saccharine style traditionally used to interpret Ancient Greece). He is kindly remembered in the role by many as "charming" and for Bakst's costume and make-up design. Bakst gave Nijinsky a most unusual lemon-coloured make-up and a blonde wig, which framed his face in flat ringlets and gave him the look of a marble statue. In Bronislava's eyes, Nijinsky looked like Michelangelo's David: "His body of the youth in love with his own image emanated health and the athletic prowess of the ancient Greek Games."

It was at least a triumph for Bakst, who was a consummate artist – a true professional who always checked the details of the costumes and make-up of each artist against his sketches before they went on stage at the premiere. The dapper dresser with a neat beard and glasses was a popular member of the Ballets Russes and a great influence on Diaghilev: he was good-natured and knew how to stand up for his own ideas and have a decisive voice. When Diaghilev was in a quandary about the worth of Nijinsky's radical choreography, it was Bakst's opinion he sought.

Petrushka was the masterpiece of the Ballets Russes – a collaboration of the inventive minds of Fokine, Bakst, Benois and Stravinsky, the creative team behind Diaghilev who were the backbone of the Ballets Russes, responsible for its early success. Stravinsky wrote the music first and collaborated on the story with Benois, who had been persuaded to forget his grievous dissatisfaction with Diaghilev and brought back to the fold to develop the concept. Benois was officially reinstated with the title of artistic director, the position he had been acting in since the beginning of the Paris theatre seasons in 1908.

Petrushka is set in a 19th-century Russian "Butter Fair" – a traditional pre-Lent fair held on Shrove Tuesday in St Petersburg, in the bitter cold of the Russian winter. It tells the story of three dolls in a travelling puppet show – Petrushka (Nijinsky), the Ballerina (Karsavina) and the Moor (Alexander Orloff) – who belong to the Old Showman (Cecchetti). The traditional puppet show was the Russian equivalent of the English Punch and Judy show and one that Benois had planned to immortalise since his childhood. The role of the pathetic puppet is said to have been Nijinsky's favourite – it had a strange synergy with his own personality, as if Fokine had seen into his soul. In rehearsals, he immediately grasped the purpose of each detail.

The ballet took Paris by storm at its premiere on 13 June 1911. The only setback was another fallout between Benois and Diaghilev over the substitution of a portrait by Bakst in the set painted by Benois. Diaghilev often overrode Benois, who was less prepared to back all his ideas. It was a casualty of the closeness of their collaboration, in which Diaghilev was often a ruthless manipulator. Benois felt justifiably "used" by Diaghilev and again left Paris. But Benois did not bear grudges and accepted Diaghilev's invitation to work with him again when he needed him for later projects. Such was the impresario's power and charm.

Many people considered *Petrushka* to be Nijinsky's finest role. Stravinsky wrote in his autobiography:

> *I should like to pay heartfelt homage to Vaslav Nijinsky's unsurpassed rendering of the role of Petrushka. The perfection with which he became the very incarnation of this character was all the more remarkable because the pure salutary work in which he excelled was in this case dominated by dramatic action, music and gesture. The ballet was greatly enhanced by the richness of the artistic setting which Benois had created for it.*

Petrushka is regarded as both Fokine's and Stravinsky's finest ballet, as well as Nijinsky's. When *Petrushka* had its London premiere, British writer Osbert Sitwell observed:

> *I have seen other great dancers, but never one inspired as was Nijinsky. I have seen other great dancers play Petrushka, but never one who with his rendering of a figure stuffed with straw, struggling from the thraldom of the puppet world towards human freedom, but always with the terrible leaded frustration of the dummy latent in his limbs, the movement of them containing the suggestion of the thawing of a winter's edge, evoked a comparable feeling of pathos. The part of Petrushka showed Nijinsky to be a master of mime, gesture, drama, just as in pure dancing, his rendering of the Spirit of the Rose in Le Spectre de la rose, was the climax of romantic ballet.*

Cyril Beaumont found Nijinsky's *Petrushka* one of the most vivid and unforgettable impressions he had ever experienced:

> *He suggested a puppet that sometimes aped a human being, whereas all other interpreters conveyed a dancer imitating a puppet. He seemed to have probed the very soul of the character with astonishing intuition. Did he in one of his dark moods of introspection feel conscious of a strange parallel between Petrushka and himself, the Showman and Diaghilev?*

It has often been suggested that Nijinsky's interpretation of the puppet was a cry for help – that Petrushka's distorted movements echoed Nijinsky's unease in life. It was a role that endorsed Nijinsky's aura of almost supernatural intrigue. As designer Grace Loval Fraser put it:

> *He was a puppet, but he suffered – you knew that he suffered, you knew all his emotions – but they were not the emotions of a human being, or a human being pretending to be a puppet. And when he died you didn't feel there was anybody inside his clothes – it was just a heap of broken bits of wood and material. How he did it, I do not know.*

It prompted Diaghilev's friend and fellow Pickwickian Walter Nouvel to ask him if he disliked Nijinsky. Why did he always give him a subordinate role of a slave or a puppet? Would he ever emancipate him? Nijinsky must have wondered himself if he would ever be free. Diaghilev was known to be excessively jealous and, from the beginning of their liaison, he had ordered his old family servant and trusted valet, Vassily, to watch Nijinsky's every move.

Vassily even interrupted Nijinsky's rehearsals, much to the annoyance of his partners and teachers, and was always amongst the throng of Diaghilev's friends and supporters who crowded the dancer's dressing room.

Later that month, the company made its London debut as part of the celebrations for the coronation of George V. Diaghilev was given the honour of producing the official gala performance on 26 June 1911 at the Theatre Royal, Covent Garden, remembered as the "hundred thousand rose performance" for the carpet of roses he arranged to completely cover the auditorium and stage. The programme for the gala included a selection of acts from three operas and a scene from *Le Pavillon d'Armide.* Subsequent programmes included *Polovtsian Dances, Scheherazade, Cléopâtre, Les Sylphides, Le Carnaval, Le Spectre de la rose* and *Le Pavillon d'Armide.*

It was all very grand and elaborate – a dream come true for Diaghilev. His company was acclaimed at the top of the ladder, both critically and socially. The season was a great success – the forerunner of many more for the company in London. The bastion of British culture was a very important city to the Ballets Russes: the season was the introduction to many of Diaghilev's most influential patrons. The company was drawn into the social festivities surrounding the coronation and invited to perform at several private parties. One of the key society hostesses, Lady Ripon, took Nijinsky under her protection and they formed a close, lasting friendship. She also introduced him to Lady Ottoline Morrell, who was associated with the Bloomsbury Group. On a later visit, the eccentric writer Lytton Strachey met Nijinsky at one of her parties and declared him "certainly not a eunuch … very nice. and much more attractive than I'd expected. As the poor fellow cannot speak more than two words of any language, it's difficult to get far with him". He was dazzled and delighted with Nijinsky as a performer and tried to make his acquaintance but was blocked by Nijinsky's bodyguard, Vassily.

When the coronation season finished at the end of July, a second six-week season was announced for later in the year, with the added attractions of two of Russia's supreme ballerinas – Pavlova in *Giselle* and Kschessinska in *Swan Lake* – both to be partnered by Nijinsky.

By the end of 1911, the Ballets Russes had restored the art of ballet in Western Europe.

Ballets like *Petrushka* were light years ahead of the insipid "entertainment" of the past. The name Diaghilev and the Ballets Russes was now a guarantee of excitement, but it represented far more than an emotional reaction: the company had made a major contribution to the arts. From its inception, the Ballets Russes was an incredible meeting place for artistic exchanges: it attracted a new audience for ballet from the brilliant society that marked the beginning of the 20th century. The Ballets Russes was at its epicentre: writers such as Marcel Proust and Jean Cocteau and composer Reynaldo Hahn were among the circus of leaders of the homosexual side of Parisian social and artistic life who were drawn to its creative energy. (Proust wrote in his seven-volume novel *A la recherche du temps perdu* – "In Search of Lost Time" of the charming invasion of the Ballets Russes, which infected Paris with a fever of curiosity.)

Diaghilev thrived on intellectual company but avidly disliked overt homosexuality and effeminate behaviour. As through the ages, Ballets Russes attracted a homosexual following to ballet, but Cocteau was the only self-confessed homosexual Diaghilev permitted into his entourage. Diaghilev's close friend and patron Misia Sert presided over one of the most gifted artistic salons Paris has ever known, and many a new work was devised under her roof. Even among the most brilliant people, conversations usually petered out and ended with all the guests paying rapt attention to Diaghilev. He was to become one of the definers of the 20th century, dominating artistic creation for the next twenty years. He was a new type of artistic leader – a visionary director who both devised the concept and shaped the complete product, paying attention to every detail. He radically altered theatre design by bringing in painters rather than decorators and commissioned some of the greatest music of the time.

Diaghilev may have been an artistic snob, always craving the new, but he was not a social snob and was regal to stagehands and society alike. He sincerely loved his artists, although it was at the expense of wanting to control their lives – he monitored their social lives, checked their invitations and would not let them drink alcohol. He was a father to the company in the authoritative Russian sense, ever conscious of his power.

BALLETS RUSSES 1912

There was a frenzy of activity for the opening season of the permanent company at the Theatre de Monte Carlo in 1912. The premieres of *Petrushka* and *L'Oiseau de feu* were scheduled as the centrepieces of the celebrations. (Fokine had difficulty remembering his own choreography for the latter and had to be reminded by Bronislava Nijinsky – showing her own colours as a promising choreographer.) Fokine had much on his mind: Diaghilev expected him to mount three new ballets for the coming fourth season in Paris, opening at the Theatre du Chatelet on 13 May.

The opening ballet was the premiere of *Le Dieu bleu* devised by Cocteau to a score by Reynaldo Hahn. As one of Nijinsky's greatest fans, Cocteau constantly lavished his praise in prose:

> *I undoubtedly have never anyone who could compare with Nijinsky and never will. I have seen him challenge the law of balance, fly straight out of the window of the Shadow of the Rose, seen him die under the snow of Petrushka and bring tears to our eyes with one gesture; I have seen him killed by a sword at the end of Scheherazade, beating the ground like a fish beats the deck of a boat. I saw him bow again and again and once more, with a sort of delightful*

> *military salute, in a storm of applause and before a raving audience that would not sit down.*

Capitalising on the taste for the Oriental, Cocteau had visualised Nijinsky at his most divine in the role of the Hindu God-King of *Le Dieu bleu*. The narrative was a Hindu story, but Hahn's music did not really fit the theme. Nijinsky appeared as an exquisite apparition, and his dancing gave the ballet some degree of success, but the choreography was dull and uninspired. Bakst's spectacular costumes and setting were the best thing about the ballet. It had only a lukewarm reception: there was little applause apart from for the opening setting.

The curtains opened on a scene dominated by a huge orange rock with protruding enormous pythons and dancers grouped in front wearing white costumes. Nijinsky was painted blue and superbly dressed in jewels and crown, performing gestures alternatively gentle and frantic. Diaghilev considered the ballet a failure, despite the *Le Figaro* critic Robert Brussel saying that Nijinsky had never appeared more marvellous than in the role of the Blue King.

Cyril Beaumont describes Nijinsky's Blue King as:

> *[a] striking, exotic-looking figure. He wore a splendidly embroidered and bejewelled blue and gold tunic, with a short stiffened skirt of oriental design and an elaborate headdress fashioned of gold wire: his face and limbs were coloured blue. His poses, for which Fokine had seemed to have taken his sources of inspiration from Hindu sculpture, were beautiful: but his role seemed to consist of posing. There was very little dancing. It was difficult to dispel the impression that for the first time Nijinsky's artistry and rare abilities had been wasted.*

The second new ballet of the season, *Thamar,* was better received, but like *Le Dieu bleu,* had only mediocre success, despite Bakst's magnificent settings for Queen Thamar's castle and the authenticity of the Caucasian costumes and dances set to the musical poetry of Mily Balakirev's magnificent score (which included his famous "Islamey" – still considered to be one of the most difficult and complicated pieces ever written for the piano).

This time, the story and setting of the ballet was in the Russian Caucasus and featured the region's traditional dances such as the Lezginka, which Thomas Nijinsky had taught his son at an early age. *Thamar* was appreciated by serious balletomanes without appealing to the general public. It was flawed by being too similar to the bacchanalian-feast-filled-with-fatal-passion theme of *Scheherazade* – without its shock quality and pizzazz.

The pressure on Fokine to produce new ballets was beginning to tell. There was far too little time and too few guaranteed resources. Now with the failure of several of Fokine's ballets in succession, Diaghilev was losing faith in him. He had become intolerant of Fokine's inability to develop his choreographic style and turned his attention to Nijinsky's choreography. Fokine felt marginalised. He believed his two new ballets were suffering from sharing the same premiere season with Nijinsky's first work, *L'Apres-midi d'un faune.*

He was hurt and insulted that *Faune* was to premiere before his own *Daphnis et Chloé,* which he had been working on since 1904 at the Imperial Ballet. Although *Daphnis et Chloé* was commissioned for the Ballets Russes 1911 season, it had been held up by Ravel's slowness with the score. Fokine also complained about a lack of rehearsal time. Diaghilev was unsympathetic to Fokine – he was aloof and preoccupied with preparing the public and the press for Nijinsky's choreographic debut. All the focus was on preparing for *Faune.*

CHOREOGRAPHER – L'APRES-MIDI D'UN FAUNE

Nijinsky was first formally invited to try his hand at choreography while he was at the Imperial School. A music student friend, Boris Vladmirovich Asafiev (who later became a leading Soviet composer), asked Nijinsky to create some dances for *Cinderella* – the opera he was producing with children of the employees of the Circuit Court. It was a pronounced success – the opera and dances were well received and Nijinsky enjoyed working with the children. Unlike his relationship with his peers, and much to their surprise, the introverted dancer had a real rapport with children. He communicated easily with them. Nijinsky was thrilled also when Asafiev asked him to choreograph his second opera, *The Snow Queen* from the Hans Christian Andersen fairy tale. It was an exercise that proved formative for his choreographic career – some of the movements Nijinsky formed for *Cinderella* he later integrated into his neoclassical work *Jeux.*

Nijinsky's choreography for *L'Apres-midi d'un faune* – his first work commissioned by the Ballets Russes – was so alien to the dancers that it took over a hundred rehearsals. He began the preliminary rehearsals in Berlin in January 1912, although the ballet did not premiere until May of that year. There was much for them to absorb: nothing could prepare either dancers or audiences for the radical new ideas Nijinsky was about to unleash.

Both Fokine and Nijinsky had been influenced by Isadora Duncan's revolutionary freedom of expression. But Fokine and Nijinsky's styles were totally opposed. Both of them were key choreographers, but despite his greatest roles being in Fokine's romantic ballets, Nijinsky rejected all "prettiness" in his own choreography. Fokine was regarded as radical by the conservative imperial regime, still loyal to the works of Petipa, but his work was dependent on spectacle and design. Nijinsky moved the art form dramatically further forward in a stark new style stripped of any artifice.

Like Fokine, Nijinsky had been inspired by the barefooted dancer to embark on a long love affair with Ancient Greece. He had been encouraged by Diaghilev to study it in detail and was intrigued by the artifacts and architecture he had seen in Greece. He spent hours studying the Elgin Marbles and the Greek vases in the Louvre and British Museum. There is little doubt that he was encouraged by his collaborators Diaghilev and Bakst – who was an authority on the period – to base the ballet on a poem by Stéphane Mallarmé to music by Claude Debussy set it in the style of the bas relief on a Greek vase.

However, the style and form of the choreography of *L'Apres-midi d'un faune* was entirely Nijinsky's own concept. It was a mammoth change in direction for the Ballets Russes and ballet in general – a contemporary work unrelated to any previous styles in classical dance. Like Fokine, Nijinsky's choreography reflected Duncan's influence in both freedom of expression and the Hellenic theme but was much more radical.

Nijinsky was the first choreographer to create a true fusion of music and movement in the mode first expressed by Isadora Duncan. American critic Carl Van Vechten wrote:

> *The choreography of Faun proves that Nijinsky's musical intelligence was of the highest order – it was the first ballet to combine the expression and flow of the music.*

Faune was a huge shock to dancers and audiences for the new principles Nijinsky introduced, which totally contradicted the traditionally turned-out position – the basis of classical ballet. There was no classical movement, no pointe shoes – it was a revolution of the art form. The choreography was based on a bare-footed, flat heel-and-toe movement, with the profile of the body turned on the side like the frieze on a vase. Nijinsky emphasised stillness and posture. It was slow-moving, almost static and grounded – there was no elevation, no legs in the air or jumping, apart from the Faun's one small goat-like leap. The style demonstrated the major difference between modern dance and ballet – it was grounded, not aerial.

Nijinsky began by trying out his ideas in secret with Bronislava as his muse, moulding her like a piece of clay. She was, luckily, enraptured by her brother's ideas and instinctively understood how to interpret them, but it was not as easy for the other dancers. There was great antagonism to the strange new choreography and, as Nijinsky was lacking in people skills, rehearsals were tense and stormy. He was naturally able to execute the movements himself but incapable of explaining them to the other dancers.

As he could only demonstrate and not explain what he wanted, Nijinsky became frustrated when the dancers failed to emulate him. They were unused to both the style and the demand for such precision of detail. Previously, choreography was much looser and only provided a framework. The ballets were open to individual interpretation as long as the dancers kept to the basic shapes, the basic grouping and the detail of the *pas*. It was the first time a choreographer had demanded precise execution of his choreography.

Rambert writes of when she was extolling the virtues of Fokine's masterpiece *Petrushka* to Nijinsky:

> *He said that it was wonderful for the three main dancers, but the (choreography of the) crowd was treated too loosely – everybody did what they wanted (Stravinsky had also been disappointed: "I regret it even more because the danses d'ensemble of the coachmen, nurses and*

mummers, and solo danced, must be regarded as Fokine's finest creations.")

Nijinsky on the contrary, did not allow the slightest freedom of movement or gesture and exacted only a perfect copy. He required a perfect ballet technique and then broke it down consciously to his own purpose – and then it proved a masterpiece. Each nymph looked like a goddess. Although they were incapable of understanding Nijinsky's intentions, the mere fact of faithfully copying his unique movements gave them the requisite style. He told them: "No expression in the face, you must be as if asleep with your eyes open – like statues."

It was a bizarre experience for the dancers, who complained that there was no dancing (as they knew it) and that they felt as if they were carved out of stone. It took Nijinsky's single-minded determination and meticulous discipline to produce the ten-minute ballet.

Even Diaghilev panicked just before the premiere and quarrelled seriously with Nijinsky for the first time, demanding he change the entire ballet. Diaghilev's conservative stance was a change of face for the entrepreneur, always ready for the new – a jettisoning of the principles that led to his resignation at the Imperial Theatre.

Nijinsky was outraged. The situation created an impasse, which was only resolved by their agreeing to ask Bakst's opinion. That vital opinion saved the ballet for the moment – Bakst thought it a "super genius" creation and the others fools for not having understood that themselves. But it was the beginning of Nijinsky's withdrawal from Diaghilev.

Fokine was an early champion of Nijinsky as a dancer and, though he had created most of Nijinsky's key roles, their relationship soured when Nijinsky began choreographing himself. Fokine was scornful of Nijinsky's new ideas and refused to refer to them as dancing. He was also a severe critic of Martha Graham and of most modern dance. He did not believe that steps alone tell a story. Indeed, *L'Apres-midi d'un faune* was not ballet in the accepted sense: the later 20th-century master choreographer George Balanchine described it as “a choreographic tableau – a moving frieze, a work to be seen only from the front. In his imitation of Greek paintings, Nijinsky was faithful to the style and to the letter; he rejected the traditional movements of classical ballet in favour of an angular rigidity that made possible a new form of expressiveness for the dancer’s body.”

Fokine did appreciate the originality of the running movements in Nijinsky’s placing of the whole foot heel-first on the ground, and he liked his use of stillness – in courageously ignoring the violent music. Although completely opposite to his own style, Fokine thought the archaic, angular choreography suited the tone of the score.

Debussy was not so sure, because Nijinsky’s use of music was another radical innovation that was very demanding of the dancers: they had to learn to keep the score in their heads and sense the rhythm in order to move between the beats.

The leading nymph was danced by Lydia Nelidova with Leokadia Klementowicz (married to fellow Ballets Russes member Adolf Bolm), Anna Tcherepanova – who died a few months later and was replaced in the cast by Lubov Tchernicheva (married to Ballets Russes *regisseur* Sergei Grigoriev) – Henryka Majcherska, Kazimiera Kopycinska, Olga Khokhlova (who later married Picasso) and Bronislava Nijinsky as the other nymphs.

One of the other early nymphs, Lydia Sokolova, who performed in the London premiere the following year in 1913, was terrified when Nijinsky told her to walk between the bars of the music and rely on sensing the rhythm. She describes the experience in her memoirs, *Dancing for Diaghilev*:

> *To be allowed to take part in Faune was an honour. The dancers had to be musical as well as rhythmical and it was necessary to relax and hear the music as a whole: it had to trickle through your consciousness and the sensation approached the divine... At every entrance one made – and there were several – one began to count, taking the count from another dancer who was coming off. For every*

> *lift of the hand or head there was a corresponding sound in the score. In order to preserve the patterns of the frieze, you had to keep your hands and arms in profile: to do this it as necessary to relax the hand and arm, for if you forced or tightened the gesture, the wrist fell back and the straight line from elbow to fingers was lost.*
>
> *Nijinsky as the Faun was thrilling. Although his movements were restrained, they were virile and powerful. The manner in which he caressed and carried the nymph's veil was so animal that one expected to run up the side of the hill with it in his mouth. There was an unforgettable moment just before his final amorous descent on the scarf, when he knelt on one knee on top of the hill, with his other leg stretched out behind him. Suddenly, he threw back his head, opened his mouth and silently laughed. It was superb acting.*

The most bizarre aspect of Nijinsky's performance was his expressionless demeanour – he was dehumanised, showing no sign of animation, his features set and deadpan. It was strange and initially unengaging, yet he was one with nature in his portrayal – an uncanny interpretation of an instinctive, quivering animal about to flee. His phallic movement at the end, which incited such outrage at the premiere and was later described by Romola Nijinsky as "an everyday act of fetishism", was a courageous display of sexual candour, which undoubtedly contributed to the ballet's success, despite the obvious outcry of moral indignation.

The role of a faun was uncannily akin to Nijinsky's own personality. Marie Rambert stated that Nijinsky's achievements as a dancer alone make him immortal. The Faun was one of Nijinsky's many inhuman roles, in which he was perceived as more than a mere mortal. Nijinsky considered his talent a gift from God. For him to perform on stage was to breathe. His feeling for the roles was the expression of his spirituality, which is why he wrote so much about feeling in his diaries, separating "feeling" people from the rest.

The premiere of *L'Apres-midi d'un faune* on 29 May 1912 turned out to be one of the most memorable in ballet history. As soon as the ballet finished, the shock of the new "style" and graphically explicit ending drew a pregnant pause – a gasp went up from the audience at Nijinsky's audacity, followed by a loud rumble of applause, mixed with protests. After all the build-up, it was so short – let alone audacious! After a few moments of confusion, Diaghilev asked Nijinsky if they could repeat the ballet. He agreed, but despite another round of loud applause, shocked dissatisfaction permeated the theatre.

No-one had seen anything remotely resembling it before – and it was in total contrast to the previous ballets of the Ballets Russes. Whereas Diaghilev had previously focused on entertainment, this ballet offered a thought-provoking new path.

When the ballet finished for the second time, the sculptor Auguste Rodin stood up in his box, calling "Bravo!" He came backstage at the interval to tell Nijinsky that the ballet was the fulfilment of his dreams. Nevertheless, *L'Apres-midi d'un faune* triggered a storm of protest. Debussy was shocked; Gaston Calmette, editor of the right-wing paper *Le Figaro*, banned the paper's critic from running his review the following morning and violently attacked the work himself:

> *Anyone who mentions the words art and imagination in the same breath must be laughing at us. This is neither a pretty pastoral work nor a work of profound meaning. We are shown a lecherous faun, whose movements are filthy and bestial in their eroticism and whose gestures are as crude as they are indecent. That is all. And the overexploit miming of this misshapen beast. Loathsome when seen full on, but even more loathsome in profile, was greeted with the booing it deserved. Our public will never accept such bestial realism.*

Calmette's outburst drew an immediate defence from Rodin, prompted by Diaghilev, in the rival paper *Le Matin*:

> *Form and meaning are indissolubly wedded in that of antique frescoes and sculpture: he is the ideal model,*

> *whom one longs to draw and sculpt. When the curtain rises to reveal him reclining on the ground, one knee raised, the pipe at his lips, you would think him a stature: and nothing could be more striking than the impulse with which, at the climax, he lies face down on the scented veil, kissing it and hugging it to him with passionate abandon. I wish that such a noble endeavour could be understood as a whole and that the Theatre du Chatelet would arrange others to which our artists might come for inspiration.*

Needless to say, the publicity produced the desired effect: extra performances had to be scheduled for all of Paris to come and see for themselves what the fuss was about.

Nijinsky had emerged as a choreographer of importance: he had introduced a whole new alphabet and vocabulary for dance – a choreographic revolution; a break with tradition and a brave attempt to create choreography that was totally new. It could not have been further from the traditional art of ballet, which Fokine had developed and liberated. It was far beyond what Diaghilev had visualised when he encouraged Nijinsky's choreography. Much as he recognised the need to progress and explore the art form, *L'Apres-midi d'un faune* catapulted it off the planet into the next age.

Dame Marie Rambert asserts in her memoir *Quicksilver:*

> *I would not hesitate to affirm that it was he, more than anyone else who revolutionised the classical ballet and was fifty years ahead of his time. Fokine was a logical development of Petipa, but Nijinsky introduced entirely new principles.*

In 1990, Ann Hutchison Guest translated Nijinsky's notation for *Faune* and revealed the clearest details of his original choreography, as opposed to the distorted versions performed in the past. She believes it to offer the most direct and compelling evidence of the innovative nature of Nijinsky's dance composition, which was so revolutionary at the time that one can understand the shock waves it created. She asserts that *Faune* is now recognised beyond dispute as an extraordinary intellectual achievement (which is a fascinating fact considering what has been said about Nijinsky's lack of intellectual ability!).

Whether or not the ballet was a "failure" at the time, Nijinsky had opened the floodgates: he had liberated dance from its traditional parameters, opening the scope and range of attitude and expression. His choreography was an essential artistic exploration: a tart reminder of the need to continuously develop the arts and allow creative people the freedom to fail. Nijinsky was the first to venture into the abstract work of modernity like cubism in painting, and his stark new movements were hated by balletomanes then as much as radical work is today.

Nijinsky's entry into the field had usurped Fokine's status as chief choreographer – he left the company in a fit of pique, aware that Diaghilev had lost confidence in his ability to develop choreographically and thought he was out of step with the new thinking and had run out of ideas.

He created further drama by accusing Nijinsky of copying his choreography, but Bronislava Nijinsky insists was the other way around. She knew that Vaslav had started to create *Faune* at the end of 1910 when he first showed it to Diaghilev and Bakst. She said that it was no surprise to her when she was told that Fokine had appropriated the style of *Faune* when he was mounting the dance of the three nymphs – the "Dance of Darkon" for *Daphnis et Chloé* – that it proved to be its most successful number.

At a later performance in Berlin, Kaiser Wilhelm complimented Nijinsky on *Faune* and afterwards sent him a copy of a bas-relief from his own collection, similar to the one Nijinsky had used as inspiration. The Kaiser was a principal patron of the company. He was reported to have demonstrated some ballet steps at a cabinet council and told his ministers, "There is more beauty in this Russian ballet than in all our museums from cellar to roof."

The company returned to London in June and July for another season, which offered almost all the ballets in its repertoire: *Thamar*; *Les Sylphides, L'Oiseau de feu, Carnaval, Le Spectre de la rose, Polovtsian Dances, Swan Lake, Le Pavillon d'Armide,*

Scheherazade and *Narcisse*. It was a feast of Fokine – and Nijinsky, whom the British critic Cyril Beaumont discovered "danced not only with his limbs but with his whole body". He "could hardly remember anything about *Swan Lake* except Nijinsky and the highlight of the season was Nijinsky as Armida's slave".

Faune was quite well received in London at the Ballets Russes next season there in February 1913, and there was less reaction to the suggestive ending than in Paris. Nijinsky was feted by London society and its most prominent hostess, Lady Ottoline Morrell. Despite his lack of social nous – once telling Lady Morrell she looked like a giraffe – Nijinsky was acknowledged there for his individuality and genius. Lady Morrell was particularly perceptive; she thought Nijinsky had the demeanour of a visitor from another world but held a darker view of his relationship with Diaghilev, who she referred to as Nijinsky's guardian and jailor.

Watching the Paris Opera Ballet perform this work – the version produced by that other famous Russian male dance icon, Nureyev – I realised the first glimmerings of the impact of Nijinsky. It is one of the most confronting ballets I've seen in the 21st century. The dancer performing the role of the Faun exhibited the animalistic character that Nijinsky originated. No other dancer I've seen in the role has ever achieved this: the role has been cut and adjusted – anything to reduce the impact of the animal sensuality Nijinsky originated almost a century ago.

JEUX

Nevertheless, Nijinsky was the man of the moment and there was much speculation about his next work – two more of his ballets were due to premiere the following season of 1913. After the impact of *L'Apres-midi d'un faune*, there was a lot of speculation. *Jeux* was yet another move away from the traditional classical ballet technique, in yet another direction. It was the first ballet to be based on a contemporary theme – specifically, that of sport, which up till then was a common subject of operettas and music hall but never ballet, which had stayed safely in themes of the past. After a lot of consideration, Nijinsky selected the socially correct sport of tennis to represent modern man. He made his final choice after coming across Virginia Woolf's brother and a friend playing tennis in Bedford Square on an evening walk with Diaghilev and Lady Ottoline Morrell. To endorse his picture of modern man, he pitched him forward to the future by setting the ballet ahead of time, in 1930.

But *Jeux* was really based on human relationships – love as revealed by a game of tennis. It was played out in a highly charged sexual tone by him, Tamara Karsavina and Ludmilla Schollar. Nijinsky said that the theme was based on a fantasy of Diaghilev's to put three men together, but he changed the sexual mix for reasons of propriety. He moved the three players as a sculpted trio, set against a summer garden background created by Bakst, again to music commissioned from Debussy.

Everything in the ballet was new – the theme, subject, music and free movements. *Jeux* is considered the first neoclassical ballet. There was no *corps de ballet*, no narrative – only an interchange of bodies in an intimate atmosphere and a complex psychological mix. It was cubist in style, projecting the radical new approach to choreography Nijinsky had begun in *Faune* further into modernity. But the ballet was coldly received and disappeared after only five performances.

The underlying sexual theme of *Jeux* was complex enough without the further complicating factor of Nijinsky falling in love with his co-star Karsavina. He had been closely associated with her since the school. She was respected as a gifted and intelligent artist, the leading female dancer of the Ballets Russes and Nijinsky's most frequent partner. Her refined, elusive style was a perfect match for Nijinsky's electrifying theatrical power. Fokine had been in love with her at the Imperial Theatre, and Diaghilev hinted on more than one occasion that he was half in love with her himself. Nijinsky wrote in his diary that he "loved her as a woman" and courted her, but she did not respond because she was married. It was an unsettling element to the comfortable relationship they had developed over the years – and a serious impediment to the development of the new ballet. They had a bad quarrel during rehearsals for *Jeux*, which Nijinsky attributed to Diaghilev's jealousy. In Nijinsky's words:

> *I could not compose Jeux. I composed this ballet on the subject of lust. The ballet was not a success, because I did not feel it. I began it well, but then they started hurrying me, and I never finished it. In that ballet you can see three young people feeling lust. I understood life at the age of twenty-two. I composed that ballet by myself. Diaghilev and Bakst helped me write down the subject of the ballet, because Debussy, the famous musical composer, insisted on having the story on paper. I asked Diaghilev to help me and he and Bakst together wrote down my story on paper. I told Diaghilev my ideas. I know that Diaghilev likes to say they are his, because he likes praise. I am*

very pleased if Diaghilev says it is he who has thought up these stories, that is the Faune and Jeux, for these ballets were composed by me under the influence of my life with Diaghilev. The Faune is me, and Jeux is the kind of life Diaghilev dreamed of. He wanted to have two boys. He often told me about this desire of his, but I showed him I was angry. Diaghilev wanted to make love to two boys at the same time and wanted these boys to make love to him. The two boys are two young girls, and Diaghilev is the young man. I camouflaged these personalities on purpose because I wanted people to feel disgust. I felt disgust, and therefore could not finish that ballet. Debussy did not like Diaghilev's idea either, but he was given 10,000 francs for that ballet and therefore had to finish it.

It took forty years for the score of *Jeux* to be recognised as one of the composer Debussy's masterpieces. After the uncomfortable experience of *Faune,* the composer had to be persuaded to write a piece of music about such an unlikely subject at the time as a game of tennis. He was initially dubious about the resulting ballet, claiming "it gave Nijinsky's perverse genius a chance of indulging in a peculiar type of mathematics". He was worried about the sexual impropriety but heartened by the fact that in ballet as he knew it, "immorality escapes through the dancer's legs and ends in a pirouette". Not in this ballet, however – there was no hint of a pirouette. Debussy appeared to later warm to the work, saying, "The perverse genius of Nijinsky has excelled in the so-called stylisation of gesture."

No doubt it was due to Diaghilev's promotional instinct that some perceptive comments on Nijinsky's choreographic philosophy were published in *Le Figaro* on the eve of the premiere of *Jeux.* The article quoted Nijinsky's comments at a lunch gathering of French and Russian artists – Diaghilev, Bakst, Cocteau, Debussy, Hahn, critic Robert Brussel, journalist Hector Cahusac and artist Jacques-Emile Blanche – in the Bois de Bologne the previous spring:

The man that I see foremost on the stage is a contemporary man. I imagine the costume, the plastic poses, the movement

> *that would be representative of our time … By attentively studying polo, golf, tennis, I have become convinced that sports are not only a healthy pastime, but also create their own plastic beauty. From studying them I drew the hope that in the future, our own time will be characterised by a style just as expressive as those antique styles we admire so much at the present.*

He fervently believed ballet themes to be ancillary to the experience of the performance itself, that as a ballet progresses, "one shouldn't have to think any more profoundly than when one is looking at a painting or listening to a symphony".

It was a significant statement from the normally reticent dancer and a conversation that had convinced Diaghilev of Nijinsky's readiness and potential to choreograph. Despite any uncertainty he had about *Faune*, Diaghilev encouraged Nijinsky's choreography for the two new ballets of the season – *Jeux* and a huge undertaking of Nicholas Roerich's concept for *Le Sacre du printemps* (which he had previously planned to give to Fokine and had commissioned Stravinsky to express some new ideas in the score).

Nijinsky was starting to contemplate serious philosophical themes and search for alternative means of expression. But like other experimental artists, he was not always able to round out his ideas. He was way ahead of his time in his search for another range of movements to display the contemporary world. He spent much time at tennis courts studying the players' arm movements but was unable to display what he wanted Karsavina and Schollar to portray in *Jeux* because he was still searching during rehearsals – he could only experiment with dance language, which was tedious for everyone involved and demanding.

Diaghilev scoffed at the barriers of tradition. In his lifelong quest for new aesthetics, he was concerned exclusively with creation and modernity at the extreme edge of the avant-garde. At the time of the advent of *Jeux*, he was championing realism.

Not much of merit is recorded about *Jeux*, which premiered on 15 May 1913, apart from the principles of Nijinsky's aims, and it has all but disappeared from dance history. At the time, there was some respect for the concept and the ballet's hints of monumental gravity, integrity, and dignity, but the public was indifferent to *Jeux*; it had little impact and the bizarre choreography blurred any recognition of Debussy's music. The high point of the ballet was reported to have been the opening, when Nijinsky jetés on stage after a tennis ball.

When it premiered in London in June of that year, Beaumont recalled an "unusual movement, which had a certain beauty from its display of muscle control, when Nijinsky turned his head to one side and tightened the muscles of his neck. The normally expressive features of the dancers were here, as in Faun, expressionless and set; doubtless this suggestion of a mask was to develop the sculptural convention".

It was never performed again. Bronislava believed that her brother had lost interest during the rehearsals and that he did not carry out his original ideas. She also blamed Bakst's designs.

> *But Jeux did live for me. I was formed as a choreographer more by Jeux and Sacre. The unconscious art of those ballets inspired my initial work. From them, I sought to realise the potential of my brother's creativity in terms of neoclassical and modern dance.*

LE SACRE DU PRINTEMPS

The next month, *Jeux* was wiped out of the conversation – and maybe the annals of dance – by the scandal of the *Le Sacre du printemps* premiere on 29 May1913. It was a turning point in the history of ballet, with the shock waves permeating down the years, both for the music and the choreography.

Le Sacre du printemps was a collaboration between Stravinsky, Nijinsky and Nicholas Roerich – a revered Russian artist who had conceived the idea of a pagan ritual of the rites of spring three years earlier and had been working on the libretto. Roerich was an academic professor and a member of the Archaeological Society, whose members specialised in depicting the life and rituals of ancient tribes. He had gained some experience in ballet when he developed the concept for the opera *Prince Igor.* Roerich spent much time speaking to Nijinsky about the theme of his paintings – the awakening of the spirit of primeval man. His designs for *Sacre* reflected a contemplative mood of a timeless epic to offset his deeply intellectual theme, which Nijinsky was determined to emulate in his choreography. The complexities of the music and subject led him to concentrate on simplicity – on depicting "the core of being" in his choreography.

He was searching for authenticity, not effect, and aimed to convey the spirit of the prehistoric Slavs and a sense of their primitive ritual through a simple pattern of continuous rhythmical stamping and jumping. But Stravinsky's music was taken from the ancient Russian peasantry and the violent, offbeat rhythms were alien to the Western ear. Prince Volkonsky, the former director of the Imperial Theatres (with whom Diaghilev had recently made up after his dramatic dismissal and its consequences to them both), recommended that they try using the Dalcroze system of eurythmics to interpret the difficult rhythms. Emile Jacques Dalcroze responded to Diaghilev's request for help by sending his prize pupil, the Polish student Cyvia (Miriam) Rambam (who later changed her name to Marie Rambert and founded her own company, Ballet Rambert – now Rambert Dance Company – in Britain). Rambert had studied with Isadora Duncan and approached dance from the perspective of both influences. The dancers nicknamed her "Rhythmitchka" but were very confused by the complexities of the eurythmics, on top of Nijinsky's demanding rehearsals. After three attempts, the lessons were abandoned. Nevertheless, Rambert stayed on to help with the ballet and afterwards joined the company. She was a great ally to Nijinsky during the stressful rehearsals – a go-between for him, the pianist, Stravinsky and the dancers and one of the few people able to develop a friendship with him because of their shared native Polish language.

Nijinsky had become fascinated by the work of modern French artists such as Gaugin, Matisse, Modigliani, Cezanne and the sculptor Rodin. After defending *Faune*, Rodin had asked Nijinsky to pose for him but disappointingly did not complete any work from the sitting. Nijinsky wrote that Rodin thought his body out of proportion; there are other theories that Diaghilev found them asleep naked together and suspected the worst. Nijinsky was trying to transpose that primitive element of the modernist's work to Russian paganism, particularly Gaugin's paintings of Tahitian women. His task was made even more challenging by the fact that it was the first time they were trying to produce a ballet about a historical period without an exact story. It was very esoteric and a huge challenge. There are no exact clues to Nijinsky's thought processes to meet the challenge of creating such a completely original work. As previously, he wiped the slate clean, emptying his mind and body of the set choreographic rules. There were none of the traditional symmetric *corps de ballet* patterns in *Sacre*. The dancers worked in separate groups across the stage, performing individual patterns of movement, pounding their feet to the off-beat rhythms in a collective mass. It was choreography of a strange and distorted genre: there was no sign of the traditional lightness, grace or beauty. The movements for both men and women dancers were uncouth and heavy, with the legs turned inwards and elbows pushed into the body with palms held flat. Nijinsky visualised a grounded pagan trance – an orgy of repetitive stamping and jumping performed by a wild mob gripped by the impulse of sun worship, capable of the violence reflected in Russia's past.

The savage, convulsive movements were possibly influenced by his observation of the insane – while he was still in Russia, Nijinsky spent a lot of time with his brother Stassik at his asylum. In struggling to represent the lifestyle of the pagan Slavs, Nijinsky's subconscious had imagined a prehistoric vision like the primitive dances of Africa and Australia – a ritual similar to the Aboriginal corroboree, which was to give insights, half a century later in the 1970s, to another major choreographer, Jiri Kylian. When Kylian asked an elderly Aboriginal man why he was dancing, the reply was, "Because my father did and his father before him and I will teach it to my son."

Bronislava and her brother shared a similar professional style. She danced in the same way and once performed *Spectre* in Nijinsky's costume – which observers found uncannily confusing. She was also on the same choreographic wavelength. It made her crucial to Nijinsky as his muse – she was one of the few dancers who could interpret his work. Nijinsky was dependent on her ability to translate his ideas into steps and transmit them to the other dancers. During the days they were working intensely together, Bronislava put off telling him her own news. She knew her brother well and, despite their closeness, dreaded his reaction to the fact that she was pregnant. As she feared, he was devastated, reacting angrily, screaming and accusing her of deliberately trying to destroy his work. He was equally accusative of her husband, Alexander Kotchetovsky; a Moscow-trained member of the company, whom Bronislava had married in London the previous July, in 1912.

It is not surprising that Nijinsky was devastated by Bronislava's news, as it affected both his new ballets – he had cast her in *Jeux* with Karsavina and himself and as the Chosen Maiden, selected by the elders to be sacrificed to ensure good harvests in *Sacre*. The Chosen Maiden's solo – the "Danse Sacrale" – in which she performs the climatic ecstasy of death is central to the work and an enormous physical and emotional challenge. Bronislava was the only dancer Nijinsky trusted to express the essence of his ideas for *Sacre*. All the other dancers loathed the ugly movements, which their trained bodies naturally rejected. Rehearsals were torture: the dancers referred to them as mathematics lessons. Their bodies kept falling back into the open, rounded movements they were used to as they struggled with the difficult rhythms of the score. They had to beat time and were annoyed by having to ceaselessly stamp in rhythm.

Nijinsky eventually replaced Bronislava in the role of the Chosen Maiden with Maria Piltz – a young dancer who was fairly new to the company. It was terrifying for Piltz, yet years later she remembered *Sacre* as the key experience of her career – tears poured down her cheeks when, as an old woman in Russia, she told of how she had been scared of the elders. Her eyes lit up when she spoke of Nijinsky, who had put her through the traumatic experience, but whom she remembered as a gentle person, although strange. There was a hint that they could have been more than friends in her account of how Diaghilev (in his extreme jealousy) had once pulled her out of a carriage she was about to ride in with Nijinsky. Nijinsky's mother and sister had hoped for a match between them and talked about it later with regret. Piltz herself left the Ballets Russes not long after Nijinsky.

Sacre was ballet in an unrecognisable form, far ahead of *Jeux* in choreographic ideas, and almost indigestible in its radical projection and emotionally exhausting musical journey. A century later, Stravinsky's score – with all its complexity and wild bar-

barism – still epitomises modernism. The music is as fresh and forceful today as when it was first composed. Excerpts are frequently used in film scores, such as Disney's *Fantasia* (1941) and the British thriller *Jade* (1995). It is often said that *Sacre* must be conducted by a Russian to instinctively feel the primeval torrent of the Russian spring. At its introduction, even the greatest of conductors relied on having Stravinsky at their side to guide them through the score. The uproar at the premiere was directed more at the music than the choreography – although the combination was a surreal experience in Paris of 1913.

The premiere of *Sacre* produced an uproar such as Paris had hardly seen – the audience was raucous and totally divided. It was a division between the establishment, who loathed modernity, and the intellectual avant-garde, who revelled in the "shock of the new." They began calling out almost as soon as the curtain went up, making a din that blocked out the music. When the dancers folded their hands on their right cheeks according to the choreography, the audience exploded, calling: "Get a doctor, a dentist, two dentists!" Marie Rambert described how one elegantly dressed woman leaned out of her box and slapped a man who was clapping, how part of the audience tried to applaud in an attempt to drown out the hissing and how it was a nightmare for the dancers: "We all desperately tried to keep time without being able to hear the rhythm." Stravinsky left his seat when it became too noisy. Montreux miraculously brought the orchestra through to the end without turning his back. Because the noise of the audience drowned out the music, Nijinsky had to stand on a chair in the wings shouting out counts to the dancers. Diaghilev ordered the lights turned up in the auditorium and, at one stage, shouted out from his box, "Let them finish the performance!" But the racket did not die down until almost the end when the Chosen Maiden began her climactic solo. When the ballet was performed in London, the Chosen Maiden's solo was interrupted several times by applause.

There was no grand reception to follow. Roerich received little attention and slipped away afterwards: Stravinsky went to a restaurant with Nijinsky and Diaghilev, who this time had courted the scandal and was satisfied with the reaction.

Although Nijinsky's choreography was dropped after its first season, it was a forceful statement of change. Choreographers today still consider *Sacre* a benchmark and continue to take up the challenge of creating their own versions set to Stravinsky's music: Stephen Page's *Rites* 1997 co-production for the Australian Ballet and his Aboriginal and Torres Strait Islander Bangarra Dance Theatre and Javier de Frutos's latest interpretation (his fourth) *Milagros (Miracles or Devotional Offerings)* in 2003 are two of many examples. As Venezuelan-born de Frutos says, "It's a work you're never really satisfied with and I wanted to approach it again from an older point of view."

Back in 1913, Stravinsky jubilantly informed the press that he had found a perfect associate in Nijinsky, who was "capable of renewing the art of ballet". But he was not consistently supportive. Diaghilev later produced a revival of *Sacre,* choreographed by his next protégé, Leonide Massine, which was more successful with audiences and that Stravinsky embraced at the time. Stravinsky then dismissed Nijinsky's choreography and remembered him only as dependent on Diaghilev. In the 1930s, he had found another "perfect associate" in George Balanchine, who was focusing on the same freedom of expression in neo-classical dance. But years later, Stravinsky again declared Nijinsky's choreography for *Sacre* to be the finest expression of his music.

DISILLUSION

Nijinsky's choreography was amazingly in advance of its time – light years removed from the traditional ballets of the Imperial Theatre ballet. It was so radical and extreme that it could only have been created by somebody unconcerned with their place in the world. Nijinsky's vision transcended all social restraints and conventions. It was an intellectual achievement and choreographic revolution. But like his previous two works, *Sacre* was, once again, too advanced for popular taste, too big a jump culturally so soon after Diaghilev's restoration of ballet, of his presenting it as a glorious spectacle and feast of the senses. It was the antithesis of ballets such as *Scheherazade. Sacre* was less entertainment than an experience.

Within two weeks, Diaghilev had presented two works that changed the course of music and ballet. In *Sacre* he had gambled on one of the most controversial works ever written: it had taken courage to present it to a public intoxicated by oriental bacchanales and femmes fatales. Yet despite the fact that these works of Nijinsky's changed the course of choreography, none of them survived in the original form in the Ballets Russes; *Faune's* ending was dramatically doctored, *Jeux* disappeared quickly from the repertoire and *Sacre* was only performed four times in Paris and three in London. It is amazing that the original choreography of *Sacre* has survived – due to Nijinsky's painstaking creation of a system of notation to record it in detail (contradicting his accusers of having little brain) and to recent researchers Millicent Hodson and Kenneth Archer, who devoted years to deciphering it and faithfully reproducing it for the Royal Ballet. It was not seen again until their reconstruction was presented by the Joffrey Ballet in 1987.

It was an illuminating example of Nijinsky's choreographic talent freed from any influences or ideas of those around him, particularly Diaghilev. Nijinsky's formidable education in the arts before he met Diaghilev is often overlooked. However much Diaghilev gloried in "educating" Nijinsky, he was no cultural ignoramus. His background had given him a strong artistic foundation – he had been exposed to the arts and artists all his life. He had performed on the dance stage from an early age and experimented with choreography for nearly as long, creating many of his own variations. He played the piano from memory and could repeat whole symphonies. As a child, he could play any musical instrument he came across and often sang opera, accompanying himself on the piano to entertain his mother's guests, but he had no patience for reading the music in front of him and found it easier to play by ear. Despite his often low academic grades, it was impossible for him to emerge from the Imperial Ballet School without a basic knowledge of culture.

Sacre was a watershed for the relationship between Nijinsky and Diaghilev. Diaghilev was disillusioned by both Nijinsky's choreography and his personality: he could no longer endure his unpredictable behaviour and violent outbursts. Although he had presented Nijinsky's groundbreaking works, Diaghilev was starting to doubt his capability as a choreographer. He had believed he could control Nijinsky's genius but was beginning to wonder – to consider the effect of Nijinsky's instability, of which he had become increasingly aware, on his creativity. The staging of Nijinsky's ballets had been torturous for everyone at the Ballets Russes, including Nijinsky himself. His lack of ability to communicate his ideas was an exhausting impediment.

Diaghilev called Bronislava to a meeting and asked her to act as a go-between for them: to tell Nijinsky that he had decided to give the next two ballets to Fokine even though one of them – *La Légende de Joseph* – had been already promised to him and Nijinsky had already started working on it with Richard Strauss. Strong undercurrents had also arisen between Fokine and Nijinsky: Fokine was fighting for his own survival and trying to secure his place back from Nijinsky. He was insisting as part of his new contract that he dance all of Nijinsky's roles himself. Diaghilev was suggesting that Nijinsky should consider taking a year off dancing.

Nijinsky had been resentful of Diaghilev's dominance for some time and had been pondering ways to engineer a break. He was tired, dispirited and resentful of his bondage. He was worn out after the strain of his three new ballets, and he could not see an end to the routine of season after season. He was becoming increasingly intolerant of his protector and tired of the relentless routine. There was much unfinished business between them: the ties between Diaghilev and Nijinsky appeared impenetrable, controlling the core of their professional lives.

In June and July of that year, London audiences had their chance to assess Nijinsky's other ballets at the premieres of *Jeux* and *Le Sacre du printemps.* Like many people, Beaumont's memory of the choreography of *Jeux* was a little hazy – it was not satisfying and made little impact. After the volatile experience in Paris, Diaghilev arranged for music critic Edwin Evans to introduce *Sacre* before the curtain went up on the opening night in London. But the audience was anxious to find out about the ballet themselves and forced the talk to be cut short. Just as it was in Paris, the audience was divided between loathing, headaches from the relentless rhythm and appreciation of the startlingly creative ideas.

Towards the end of June 1913, the company finished the London season and began preparations for its first tour across the Atlantic. Much to everyone's surprise, Diaghilev made some pretext for not going on the tour. His excessive superstition had caused him to avoid sea trips since a gypsy had prophesied that he would die on the water. It was possibly also influenced by his own uncertainty about his future with his emotionally unpredictable star. Whatever the reason, it was an extraordinary decision considering the importance of the company's first trans-Atlantic tour. For the same reason, it was a relief to Nijinsky. Little did he realise how much it was about to alter his fate.

Nijinsky Children: Vaslav, Bronislava, Stanislav

Nijinsky in Practice Clothes early1900's

Signed portrait of Vaslav Nijinsky 1909

Performing Pavillion D'Armide, 1909 with Anna Pavlova

As Count Albrecht in Giselle 1910

Partnering Tamara Karsavina in Giselle

Diaghilev, Nijinsky and Stravinsky

Nijinsky and Diaghilev

Leon Bakst, Diaghilev, Nijinsky and two unidentified women

Nijinsky as The Golden Slave in Scheherazade, 1911

Nijinsky in Le Dieu Bleu, 1912

Drawing of Nijinsky in Le Spectre de la Rose by John Singer Sargent

Nijinsky with Maurice Ravel

Maurice Ravel, Vaslav and Bronislava Nijinsky

Nijinsky in Le Spectre de la Rose1911

Bronislava and Valsav Nijinsky in Apres Midi d'un Faune 1912

Vaslav Nijinsky and Igor Stravinsky, 1911

Nijinsky in the title role of Petroushka 1912

Romola and Vaslav's Wedding in Buenos Aires, 1913

Vaslav Nijinsky with his daughter Kyra1916

Nijinsky studying the score of Till Eulenspiegel, 1916

Nijinsky making up artist in Till Eulenspiegel, 1916

Romola and Vaslav, 1916

ROMOLA

During a season in Budapest the previous year, Nijinsky had taken the eye of a young Hungarian aristocrat, Romola de Pulszky. Romola was engaged to be married to a suitable young man – Baron Hatvany Bandi (Andras), whose wealthy industrial family had purchased their title and extensive estates. It was not a love match but a relationship encouraged by their families, particularly Bandi's mother. She invited Romola to accompany her to the opening night of the Ballets Russes at the Opera House in Budapest.

Romola was transfixed, feasting her eyes on the brilliant spectacle, lavish scenery and mesmerising performance. Her only disappointment was when told that she had not seen the major star. Noting her fascination, the baroness invited her again the following night.

Romola was infatuated from the moment she set eyes on the "God of dance." In her biography of Nijinsky, Romola describes how, the first time she saw "the slim, lithe, cat-like Harlequin" enter the stage, "an electric shock passed through the entire audience. Intoxicated, entranced, gasping for breath, we followed this superhuman being ... This magnificent being was Nijinsky". It was the moment she became perhaps the world's first dance groupie:

> *My one desire, from that moment on, was to know more about the extraordinary manifestation of art embodied*

in this entire company and the individuals who had succeeded in creating it.

Romola had decided she wanted Nijinsky for herself. She was immersed in drama and had been studying the art form as her mother was a famous star of the theatre stage. Overnight her focus changed to dance. She was aided by the fact that her mother was a cultural celebrity who kept an open house and was in the habit of inviting visiting artists to her salon. Emilia Markus was Hungary's leading actress – the Sarah Bernhardt (who was bewitching Paris stages at the time) of Hungary. It was not difficult for Romola to engineer an introduction to members of the Ballets Russes. Her mother's cultural contacts soon turned up a connection with Adolf Bolm, one of the leading dancers – whose forte was roles such as the Warrior Chief in *Prince Igor*. Romola wasted no time in inviting him to the salon. Through Bolm she met other members of the company and gradually infiltrated it, but it was not easy to make the acquaintance of its star.

Nijinsky's personality kept him aloof and his relationship to Diaghilev removed him even further from the rest of the company. Diaghilev guarded Nijinsky jealously and had instructed his valet Vassily to watch over him at all times. It was immensely disappointing to Romola that she had failed to make contact with her idol by the end of the season. She was forced to bide her time until the company returned to Budapest for a second season the following Christmas.

Romola was showing signs of her future tenacity and completely devoted herself to the cause. She spent as much time as possible with the Ballets Russes, attending every performance, and managed to inveigle her way into watching every rehearsal – including the inner sanctum of the daily ballet class – by cultivating an acquaintance with Maestro Cecchetti, whom she had met through Bolm.

Given such determination, it was inevitable that she would eventually achieve her goal. Not that it achieved much when she was eventually introduced to Nijinsky at a rehearsal. Apart from his natural introspection, there was also the barrier of language.

Romola was an accomplished linguist and could speak Hungarian, English, French and German, but not Polish or Russian. The lack of language caused an immediate misunderstanding – Nijinsky mistook her for a Hungarian prima ballerina whose name was mentioned in their brief conversation. He was courteously charming when they next met, although they were unable to speak directly, but later aloof – probably after being told that he had mistaken her identity.

Unabashed, Romola followed the company to Vienna to continue her siege. With the help of another family contact, the influential Hungarian music critic, Ludwig Karpath, she managed to convince Diaghilev of her commitment to become a dancer and persuaded him to let her take a class with Cecchetti. Amazingly, at the beginning of February 1913, Romola de Pulszky joined the Ballets Russes. How did she reach that level of expertise so quickly?

It was a major breakthrough in her quest to become closer to the "God of the Dance". She was able to continue her stalking at closer quarters and enlist the aid of dressers at the theatre and maids at the hotels. Her major accomplice was her own maid, Anna, with whom she shared all her confidences and discussed the daily progress of her hoped-for affiliation with the "God". Romola's engagement to Bandi had never carried conviction and was well buried, as indeed he showed signs of being gay. The only serious sadness was felt by his family. Romola prayed a lot for the fulfilment of her quest for her icon, the Little Jesus of Prague.

For eighteen months, she tracked Nijinsky around Europe. Anna was kept busy searching for sightings and planning strategies to realise her mistress's dream. One time, she succeeded in obtaining tickets for a compartment next to Diaghilev and Nijinsky on the train, an opportunity which Romola maximised by forcing a brief encounter and exchange of words (mostly on her part) in the corridor. Anna's eventful major triumph was in securing cabins on the same deck as Nijinsky on the ship taking the company on tour to South America. It was becoming a costly exercise, which Romola disregarded, exhibiting her natural extravagance by upgrading her *corps de ballet* second-class ticket to first class with her own funds.

On 15 August 1913, the Ballets Russes embarked on the SS *Avon*, en route to Buenos Aries. Diaghilev was not there to say goodbye. For different reasons, Diaghilev's absence was a window of opportunity for both Nijinsky and Romola: a bonus of twenty-one Diaghilev-free days.

Neither of them wasted a moment: Nijinsky intended to maximise his time to himself, but Romola quickly found the spot on deck where Nijinsky did his class. She luxuriated in the chance to be near her idol and observe his creative process, making it her business to be there each day trying to develop a conversation in French – their only means of spoken communication. Nijinsky had some grasp of it as the language of dance and from his seasons in Paris. Romola also spent time building a relationship with Nijinsky's masseur by enduring a lot of conversations about muscles.

During this time, Nijinsky was engrossed with other issues; in his mind, he had classified the starstruck girl as among the anonymous mass of his fan following. Since the Budapest season in the spring of the previous year, Nijinsky had been through the most momentous period of his career: he had worked prodigiously as principal dancer of the Ballets Russes and choreographed three ballets – *Faune* in May 1912 and both *Jeux* and *Sacre* in May 1913. Unlike Fokine, he was not able to stop dancing while he was choreographing: his performances were essential for the company's success. He was burnt out from the enormous pressure he had been under professionally and the growing dissatisfaction he was harbouring with his personal life.

But work was his panacea, and Nijinsky was taking the opportunity onboard the ship to work on new ideas. He had discussions before he left with Richard Strauss, whom Diaghilev had commissioned to compose the score for a ballet of the story on the religious theme of the shepherd boy and King Potiphar's wife, *Joseph and Potiphar* (later changed to *La Légende de Joseph*). Count Harry Kessler and Hugo Hofmannsthal had written the libretto, and Nijinsky was to both create the choreography and perform the role of Joseph. He did not know of Diaghilev's intention to transfer the work to Fokine. He was also nurturing an idea of choreographing a ballet of pure movement to match the pure music of Bach, which he was working on daily with the conductor for the tour, Rhené-Baton.

Although he showed no sign of encouragement, Nijinsky began to tolerate Romola's presence. Deep in his mind, he was beginning to form an idea.

CHANGE OF ROLES

Diaghilev, in his absence, had appointed the Ballets Russes sponsor Baron Dmitri de Gunzburg in his place as director of the company for the tour. Gunzburg was a dilettante, balletomane and amateur painter. He was also a friend of Romola's parents and had promised to look after her on the trip. Little did they realise that Gunzburg would be the go-between in the most important decision of her life.

The day before they were due to arrive at Rio de Janeiro, Romola successfully engineered a brief encounter with Nijinsky. On meeting him in the corridor, she confessed to having taken a little cushion as a keepsake some weeks before. Romola may or may not have known it had been given to him by his mother but used it as a ruse to speak to him. She offered to give the cushion back, but Nijinsky acted dismissively, telling her to keep it.

Later that day, Romola was confronted by Gunzburg, who said he had to speak to her urgently: in the absence of a properly shared language, he had been commissioned by Nijinsky to ask for her hand in marriage. Much as they were the words of her dreams, Romola was completely shocked. It was her heart's desire to be closer to her idol, but they were nowhere near that in her view, and it is unlikely that she ever imagined that they would marry. Gunzburg's announcement was so unexpected that she thought that she was being made fun of. She ran off and hid in her cabin.

When she finally emerged for a walk on deck later that night, she was horrified to run straight into Nijinsky. Without any preamble, he immediately asked, "*Mademoiselle, voulez vous, vous et moi?* [Will you, you and me?]" pointing to the ring finger of her left hand in theatrical mime style.

"*Oui, oui, oui!*" she replied.

She was completely in shock. When she woke the next day, Romola thought it must have been a dream, but the reality was confirmed when Gunzburg contacted her early, on instructions from Nijinsky. He wanted to buy her a ring on their port of call the next day – the company stopover in Rio de Janeiro.

Having taken action, Nijinsky was apparently keen to clinch their agreement. The newly affianced couple spent the day sightseeing and buying wedding rings, which Nijinsky arranged to have engraved *Vaslav – Romola 1/9/1913*. When the news leaked out to the company later in the day, the artists, who had been bewildered by the presence of the "socialite" on board, were shocked and terrified. Nijinsky and Romola had hardly been seen together and had certainly not been contemplated as a couple. In her biography of Nijinsky, Romola describes a conversation she had with her friend Adolf Bolm. Bolm was aghast at Romola committing herself to someone he had not known her to be interested in: "A man you don't know – a perfect stranger – a person you can't even talk to."

"But I know Nijinsky," she replied. "I have seen him dancing many, many times. I know his genius, his nature, everything."

As Gunzburg had promised Romola's parents that he would look after her, he felt duty-bound to warn her that "Nijinsky's relationship with Diaghilev is more than a friendship. He can't possibly be interested in you, and it will ruin your life".

It was an odd disclaimer from Gunzburg, considering the part he played as catalyst in the affair. Nevertheless, whatever Romola chose to believe about her fiancé's relationship with Diaghilev, she replied to him that she would "be happy serving Nijinsky's genius".

With Baron Gunzburg at the helm, the situation took on its own momentum. He arranged the wedding in haste, dispatching telegrams to Romola's mother for permission, as she was under age, but strangely, not to Nijinsky's mother, despite his closeness to her (he still wrote to her every day), or to Diaghilev. To Romola, there was an air of incredulity; to the dancers, there was a feeling of impending doom. They were terrified of Diaghilev's reaction. Several of them, like Marie Rambert, were in love with Nijinsky themselves. She was more successful than anyone else at drawing him out of himself. One of her protégés, Christopher Bruce, former director of the London-based Rambert company, tells of her recounting how her tears fell into the trunk in her cabin when she heard the shocking news of the engagement. Lydia Sokolova says, in her book *Dancing for Diaghilev*, "If Mim (as Rambert was familiarly known) had been given the chance, she could have done more than anyone else to keep him sane and happy."

On 10 September 1913, Romola de Pulszky and Vaslav Nijinsky were married at the city hall of Buenos Aires in a ceremony of mixed languages – Nijinsky gave his vows in Russian and Romola in Hungarian and French; the mayor's address was in Spanish, which neither understood. It was followed by a church ceremony at the fashionable Iglesia St Miguel that was conducted in Latin and Spanish and was equally incomprehensible to them both.

There was little time to ponder their union, as they were both taking part in the dress rehearsal that day for the opening of their season at the Teatro Colon – Buenos Aires's beautiful old opera house. Romola made her debut in the company by falling prone on stage. Nijinsky was immeasurably disappointed to discover that his new wife had no talent for dance:

> *I asked her to learn dancing because for me, dancing was the highest thing in the world after her ... I wanted to teach her good dancing, but she became frightened and no longer trusted me.*

Romola was more flabbergasted when her new husband looked at her without any sign of recognition during a performance of *Swan Lake* a few days later: she had not understood that, true to form, he had metamorphosed into his role. He was the Prince, not the person Nijinsky.

It was a serious oversight to have not obtained agreement for the wedding from either Diaghilev or Eleonora – there had been time enough in the ten-day gap after the engagement to send and receive telegrams over the ship's radio. The news was sent the next day – the same day as the opening performance at the Teatro Colon. Bronislava could not understand her brother not letting his mother know, considering how much he cared for her. Much later, Romola told her: " I am not stupid. To give advance notice of our wedding plans to Diaghilev or Vaslav's family and risk you stopping us …."

There are mixed accounts of who was the prime mover in engineering such a swift marriage. One wonders why Gunzburg, as Diaghilev's deputy, did not see it as his duty to inform the director of the company. Bronislava believed Gunzburg was trying to remove Nijinsky from the Ballets Russes and from Diaghilev's favours; there was another story of Gunzburg having aspirations of taking over from Diaghilev and plotting to sever the relationship between the impresario and his lover. Richard Buckle reported in *Diaghilev* that Gunzburg wanted to start a new company with Nijinsky. Whatever the reasons, it marked the end of that era of rich, innovative partnership and undoubtedly contributed to Nijinsky's personal demise.

Contrarily, Nijinsky showed no sign of the preoccupied performer in their private life. Every morning, he courted Romola with a large bunch of white roses. She, in turn, declared their physical union to be "her offering on the altar of happiness". But to her dismay, she almost immediately became pregnant. The lover of Diaghilev had abruptly transformed to the role of husband and now to prospective father. However, he was horrified when Romola arranged to terminate the pregnancy and greatly relieved when she changed her mind. His sensitivity was so extreme that when Romola was unwell one day, he felt sick himself. He elected to stay with her that night instead of going to the theatre, despite desperate pleas from management.

He also missed a performance in Rio de Janeiro – this time, deliberately, to force payment of money Diaghilev owed him. It was a delicate issue, as Diaghilev had formed an unconventional arrangement with Nijinsky early in their relationship. It served his unstable financial position to not pay Nijinsky any salary but to take care of his expenses – his accommodation and restaurant bills, as well as his clothes and ballet shoes. Nijinsky's privileged position as Diaghilev's amour gave him a comfortable lifestyle, and a contract had been considered a mere formality. In the ways of the old social protocols, Diaghilev also sent money to Nijinsky's mother, Eleonora, for her living expenses and rent in St Petersburg. Nijinsky had recently begun to query the arrangement, and Diaghilev had promised him that he would receive a lot of his back pay in South America. Like many of Diaghilev's promised payments to creditors, it did not happen. Now that Nijinsky had formed forces with Romola, the balance of his relationship with Diaghilev shifted dramatically. Romola exerted her influence on her husband for the first time by encouraging him to go on "strike" for a night to enforce his payment. Gunzburg had no option but to find the money.

Meanwhile, back in Europe, Diaghilev had decided Nijinsky's ballets had failed. In a desperate bid to regain audiences, he had been negotiating with Fokine to reinstate him. Diaghilev's need offered Fokine the upper hand: in a five-hour conversation, he used all his bargaining power to oust Nijinsky from the Ballets Russes and demanded that he perform all Nijinsky's roles himself.

DISASTER

Nijinsky's life had been tied to Diaghilev for so long – and so intensely – that it was a huge shock to Nijinsky when Diaghilev was not there to meet him on his arrival back in Europe. The full consequences of his actions had yet to dawn on him. The newly married couple headed towards Nijinsky's family in Russia, stopping in Budapest to see Romola's parents on the way. They were feted en route by friends and relations, but it was a period of suspended animation, as they had not yet faced Diaghilev's reaction. Nijinsky had written his former lover a long letter of explanation, naively assuming that nothing would change. He confirmed his commitment to the company and waited for word.

The blow came when they were staying with Romola's parents: Nijinsky received a telegram not from Diaghilev, but the company manager/*regisseur* Serge Grigoriev on his behalf: Mr Diaghilev had instructed him to tell him that his services were no longer required. He had been dismissed for failing to perform on tour according to his contract. Nijinsky was sacked for the second time in his career. More than that, he was dropped by his major friend, motivator and agent. Nijinsky had been under the patronage of the rich and influential since entering the Imperial School, particularly since his liaison with Prince Lvov. He had led a sheltered life, obeying orders and focusing on his art. For the first time in his adulthood, he was rudderless – without a protector.

It was a devastating blow on all sides. Diaghilev's jealousy was legendary and Nijinsky, in his naivete, had not thought through the scenario; Romola wondered if she had made a mistake in marrying an idol – a man whom she hardly knew. It was an ominous beginning to their married life. They had been worried about, yet unprepared for, such a drastic reaction from Diaghilev. Diaghilev was very wounded: he had lost his closest friend, one of the few people to whom he had revealed his tender, human side. He had also lost the star of his company, his unique discovery – his puppet? Even Grigoriev doubted that Nijinsky could be replaced: the Ballets Russes repertoire had been largely built around him.

Diaghilev's fortune was at risk as well as his emotional health – he was dependent on those who could interpret the fruits of his fertile imagination. Diaghilev loved Nijinsky, and although their intimate relationship was drawing to a close, his action was deduced to be driven by a mixture of jealousy and anger that he had not dictated. He felt tricked and humiliated. Although essentially a creator, he was partly a tyrant, accustomed to controlling every detail of his operation and everything relating to the previously compliant dancer.

It was a career crisis for Nijinsky. He was an outcast from the only way of working, and the only kind of people, that he knew. He had been sheltered by the theatre community all his life: although the best dancer on offer in the Western world, he was unequipped for freelance work and dysfunctional without a supporting network.

To Nijinsky and Romola's surprise, he was not immediately overwhelmed by counteroffers. Nijinsky had never been political, was not a social operator and had no business savvy. Great dancer that he was, the European theatre world was more in awe of Diaghilev.

The Paris Opera offered Nijinsky the role of ballet master and *premier danseur*, but he was unhappy with its repertoire and well aware that teaching was not his forte. There were few alternatives. He would have to face military service if he returned to Russia, and even if the Imperial Ballet would have him back, he would be bored by the restrictions of the repertoire and the conservative regime. Eventually, the pressure of having to support an expectant wife, as well as his mother and brother in Russia, forced Nijinsky to sign a contract with Alfred Butt, the owner of a vaudeville theatre – the Palace, in London. It was the theatre where Anna Pavlova had been performing for several years. Nijinsky was to produce an eight-week season of ballet in a varied programme of other acts. Butt undoubtedly hoped Nijinsky would be a drawcard to a new sector of the ticket-buying public, but there was no guarantee of success – the audience of the Palace was not attuned to classical music or ballet.

Nijinsky made plans to form a company and choreograph some new works for the programme as well as present those he already knew. Bronislava had resigned from the Ballets Russes in support of her brother. She and her husband Alexander Kotchetovsky formed the nucleus of the new company and were invaluable in helping Nijinsky organise the season. He could have not managed without her. Bronislava and Kotchetovsky travelled to Russia to recruit other dancers, which was not easy – most dancers were reluctant to be prised away from their regular work for a mere eight-week season, but they eventually managed to put together a company of ten women and four men.

SAISON NIJINSKY

Saison Nijinsky was ill-fated from the start. Nijinsky was out of his depth: he was totally ignorant of company management and artistic direction – both were right out of his sphere. He had no awareness or experience of that side of the business, which required skills he did not understand or possess. Things began to go wrong from the beginning.

Nijinsky planned to present a programme of his own ballets: *L'Apres-midi d'un faune, Le Spectre de la rose* and his own versions of *Carnaval* and *Les Sylphides* plus some new short works. As the pièce de résistance, Maurice Ravel had agreed to work with him on a new orchestration of *Les Sylphides* to the music of Chopin.

The first blow was to be turned down by Bakst, whom he was relying on to help with the designs. Bakst had been instructed by Diaghilev not to have anything to do with Nijinsky. It was the first of many obstacles to Nijinsky's new venture by the people who had formed his previous life: Fokine tried to protect his rights to *Le Spectre de la rose* and prevent Nijinsky from performing it, Diaghilev filed for breach of contract against Bronislava and Pavlova sent Nijinsky a bitchy telegram, sarcastically congratulating him on becoming a music hall artist as a comeback for remarks he had made to her years before that she had never forgiven about choosing to be a music hall artist rather than a *prima ballerina* of the Ballets Russes. There was very little time to prepare for the season, and the dancers spent almost all the hours of the day in rehearsal, the new sets for *Faune* were ruined by clumsy handling of fireproofing liquid and to cap it off, on opening night, Diaghilev himself showed up and unsettled Nijinsky by plonking himself in the middle of the front row of the audience.

His London friends had rallied: supporters such as Lady Rippon, Lady Morrell, and Emilia Markus and her second husband Oscar Pardany travelled from Budapest for the opening, but the odds were loaded against a spectacular success. The critics who had previously lauded Nijinsky were now lukewarm in their reviews. Beaumont writes of a general feeling of disappointment in Nijinsky's performance, of missing "the mystic fragrance" that had previously surrounded his dancing, that "he still danced with that rare elevation and feeling for line and style … but no longer danced like a god". With so many new elements of increased pressure and responsibility to deal with and a less spectacular setting than the Ballets Russes, it was hardly surprising that Nijinsky was not in top form.

He was outraged when Butt demanded more Russian content be added to the show. Butt's lack of appreciation of the high artistic values Nijinsky was struggling to produce provoked him into a violent reaction, but he did substitute the stirring *Polovtsian Dances* for one of the more classical items when he calmed down.

Worse was to come when there was discord over the music played between acts: Nijinsky objected to the music hall custom of continuous "entertainment". It was because audiences became restive while they were waiting for the stage set to be changed over for ballet between the vaudeville acts. Nijinsky had asked the pianist to play something appropriate, but he was furious when he heard music by Tchaikovsky being played instead of Carl Maria von Weber's overture to *Le Spectre de la rose.* He became distraught and beyond reason, screaming and raging. He threw his costume on the floor and refused to prepare for the ballet. In desperation, the stage manager called Bronislava. She managed to persuade Nijinsky to calm down sufficiently to continue dressing and perform the ballet, but it was very unnerving for everyone concerned. It was a particularly disturbing experience for Bronislava, who never could have imagined that inglorious occasion would be the last time she saw her brother dance.

The next day, Nijinsky was ill with a fever. Chaos reigned as the dancers, some of whom were inexperienced, were forced to improvise the gaps left in the new ballets of the second programme. Nijinsky's understanding of his contract was that it allowed him to miss three days of performances, and he accordingly prepared to drag himself out of his sickbed for the fourth night, but it was to no avail – Butt had cancelled Saison Nijinsky.

As Nijinsky could not read or speak English, he had probably misunderstood the intricacies of the contract. The season was a financial and public relations disaster. Once again, and for the fourth time in his career, Nijinsky was dismissed, sacked. To his credit, he made it a point of honour to find the money to pay the dancers after the experience of his own financial struggle with Diaghilev. It was a dismal end to the first independent professional experience for the God of the Dance. In his diary, Nijinsky refers to it in drastic terms: "Butt wants to force me to pay damages for an unfulfilled contract, whereas my work for him cost me my life."

REPLACEMENT

On the way home, Nijinsky courageously stopped in Paris to attend the premiere of *La Légende de Joseph,* which was to have been his next project. Once again, Nijinsky's trusting simplicity rebounded. When he visited the box of the Diaghilev entourage at the interval, he was treated with disdain. He was ignored by some of his former associates and coldly reprimanded by his former fawning fan Cocteau for choosing the role of husband and father. Cocteau added the final barb: "How utterly disgusting is birth."

It was also the debut of his replacement – Diaghilev's new protégé, Léonide Massine, who had been allocated Nijinsky's professional role in the ballet and in Diaghilev's personal life. Massine was a beautiful-looking eighteen-year-old whom Diaghilev had spotted on the Bolshoi Theatre stage.

Massine had been about to leave ballet to concentrate on drama and had no intention of accepting Diaghilev's unsolicited offer, but such was the maestro's power that, by the end of their meeting, Massine found himself agreeing to join the Ballets Russes.

Massine was intelligent and good-looking with a strong personality and great flair for theatricality but was not a technically accomplished dancer. He was thrust into the hands of Cecchetti to work on his technique. He became an interesting performer but never a classicist – which was reflected in his futuristic choreography.

Massine carried much of the success of the immediate postwar years of the Ballets Russes as principal dancer and choreographer. His focus was on the style and drama of dance. He choreographed some very successful ballets for the company and was a key contributor to its revival after the First World War. Chief among his creations were *Le tricorne* or "*The Three-Cornered Hat*" (which was designed by Picasso), *La Boutique fantasque, Pulcinella* (with Pergolesi's music recomposed by Stravinsky, also designed by Picasso) and a new version of *Le Sacre du printemps* in 1920 with Lydia Sokolova in the leading role of the Chosen Maiden.

Ironically, Massine also became hungry for his independence and, in 1921, committed the mortal sin of falling in love with one of the dancers. Sokolova recalled: "Even though flirting with him was against the rules, many of the women had a crush on him – although no-one seemed to 'penetrate his frozen stare'." They were all amazed when Massine began to flirt with "the company seductress" Tchernicheva, Grigoriev's wife. After seeing them together at a reception, the flirtation was put a stop to by Diaghilev. When Massine became further involved with another dancer, Vera Savina, whom he later married, Diaghilev dismissed him immediately – as he had Nijinsky – before Massine had time to take any action himself.

Diaghilev was attracted by Nijinsky and Massine's reluctant bisexuality and, in Massine's case, by his intellect. Massine was the only one of his dancer lovers on an equal level in his cultural circle and the one he mourned the most.

OFFSTAGE

On 19 June 1914, in Vienna, Romola gave birth not to the son they both wanted but to a daughter – Kyra (Russian for "queen") Vaslovovna (in honour of her father) Nijinskaya. The baby physically resembled her father. Nijinsky quickly recovered from his disappointment and became besotted with his offspring. He had always related to children and spent hours caring for his own baby.

It was hard for him not to be performing – Nijinsky had never experienced a prolonged period offstage. Meanwhile, in London, Lady Ripon was determined to reconcile the star with the company and exerted all her influence on Diaghilev. When the resulting longed-for call came to join the Ballets Russes in London just two weeks after Kyra's birth, Nijinsky agreed to dance a few performances of the season.

But he had not bargained for the dancers' reaction to his changed circumstance. The shift of power from untouchable ownership by Diaghilev to artist of the past had altered his status within the company. He was made to feel uncomfortable and unwanted. Sensitive soul that he was, Nijinsky returned to Romola and the baby without setting foot on stage. It was said at the time that he received a telegram from her demanding his immediate return, but there is doubt over whether this was the truth.

Nijinsky longed to return to Russia. Diaghilev's hopes of a Ballet Russes season in its home country had continually failed. In 1911, Diaghilev had booked the People's Palace in Narodny Dom and contracted extra performers for the season, including Mata Hari. A month before they were due to open, Narodny Dom was burnt to the ground and Diaghilev was unable to find another theatre big enough to house the company, apart from the Mariinsky. That was out of the question both politically and physically, as it was the middle of the winter season of the Imperial Ballet. It was only one of the many obstacles he encountered in his quest.

Time had passed since Nijinsky's last call-up for military service, and the break with the company offered the opportunity Nijinsky had been waiting for during the three years of his absence from the country. Now he had little Kyra to introduce to her grandmother in St Petersburg. Excitedly, the new family made plans for their trip, deciding to stop in Budapest on the way to visit Romola's family. Their timing could not have been worse: on 1 August 1914, during their sojourn in Budapest, Russia and Germany announced that they were at war. A few days later, France and England joined the battle. The borders closed and, despite all Romola's attempts, the family was marooned in Budapest, caught by the outbreak of the First World War.

It was not long before there was a knock on the door from the Hungarian police. As a Russian citizen, Nijinsky was an alien: he was under orders to be placed under arrest and interned in a prisoner-of-war camp with his wife and daughter. Romola was furious: how could they treat her husband like this – a former soloist of the tsar? She threw herself into utilising all her high-powered Markus/de Polsky contacts. After frenetic, lengthy lobbying, the authorities were somehow persuaded to commute their orders from camp internment to house arrest. The Nijinskys had escaped the deprivation of life at camp but were still civil prisoners of war, unable to leave the country. Life was looking very bleak: their relationship with Romola's mother, Emilia Markus and Oscar Pardany, was uneasy. They were devastated to be forced into dependence on them, as they were running out of money.

DEPRESSION AND CREATION

It was an ineffable situation for them all: Nijinsky was a pacifist, unable to accept the state of war, and Romola's mother was uneasy about harbouring a Russian son-in-law under her roof. She reportedly worried that it could be detrimental to her public identity and career.

It is hardly surprising that Nijinsky became depressed. He was bored in Budapest and wrote later that he thought Emilia Markus was a hypocrite: "I can understand why my wife's first husband shot himself." The season in London had drained him psychologically and caused his physical collapse. Apart from the baby and Romola, he was bereft of creative outlets and all else he held dear. He was an outcast from his beloved Russia and the two people he was closest to – his mother and sister. He was at the height of his creative powers and ill-equipped to exist without a focus. His life had always been scheduled, and he was unaccustomed to having time on his hands. He loved spending much of it with his baby daughter and had taken over a lot of her care. Nijinsky lavished his artistic talents on Kyra – decorating her bedroom with his paintings and making her toys. But the baby's bedroom was hardly a substitute for the theatres of the world.

It was a sanguine idea of Romola's to think of appealing for help from her cousin, Lily de Markus, who was an accomplished concert pianist. She gradually drew Nijinsky out of his depression by playing for his barre exercises and exploring possible music to match the choreographic ideas with which his fertile mind was churning. For some time, he had been interested in choreographing a ballet with a medieval theme and was listening to German gothic music. Having been thwarted in his first attempt to work with Richard Strauss on *La Légende de Joseph*, Nijinsky began to plan a new ballet to his tone poem *Till Eulenspiegel*, based on the German and Flemish legend of the prankster Till – a comment on the society of the time. Strauss admired Nijinsky and had been disappointed when *Joseph* was taken away from him. Nijinsky studied the folk dances of the Middle Ages for ideas to incorporate into the choreography and immersed himself in the paintings and engravings of Albrecht Durer, whose depictions of life in the German Renaissance inspired him with their rich and sometimes grotesque detail.

Nijinsky had almost completed a ballet to Liszt's *Mephisto-Walzer,* focusing on Faust and Mephistopheles, which was a stylised image of friendship in a medieval form. He was also thinking about a Japanese ballet based on Hokusai paintings.

Nijinsky also worked at developing his system of notation – a form of symbols written on musical staves – to record the new movements of his choreography, which was impossible with the Stepanov method traditionally used in Russia. It was a shock when he received another knock on the door by the police. Someone had informed the military authorities that Nijinsky spent his time drawing lines of strange symbols; it took some time to convince them that he was not a spy and the symbols were not some sort of code.

REPRIEVE

After about a year of restricted living, the Nijinskys received a message that Diaghilev was trying to contact them about a tour to America. It was the lever Nijinsky and Romola were looking for to persuade the military authorities to let them leave Budapest. In January 1916, they were permitted to leave Hungary for Vienna, where they discovered that many other people had been lobbying for their release. Diaghilev had used all his influence to free Nijinsky. The list included such high-powered names as the King of Spain, the Pope, Franz Joseph of Austro-Hungary and leaders of society and culture throughout the rest of Europe and Great Britain such as Lady Ripon and Strauss, who met with Nijinsky in Vienna to discuss *Till.* Strauss offered to adapt his score for the choreography, but Nijinsky was happy with it as it was. Nijinsky meticulously followed Strauss's scenario and music in his production and he was happy with Nijinsky's treatment.

After a short period of luxuriating in the comparatively affluent environment of Vienna, the Nijinskys were called to the American embassy to be told that their release as prisoners of war had been finally sanctioned and they were free to leave for America. Diaghilev had also suffered during the war and, in 1914, had been forced to disband the company. There was obviously little chance of work in Europe for the Ballets Russes. It had taken Diaghilev a lot of negotiating to arrange the trip to America in a contract with the Metropolitan Opera House in New York. One of the conditions was that its stars – Nijinsky and Karsavina – would perform with the company. Diaghilev was forced to accept, but Karsavina was not well, and it was a daunting task to secure Nijinsky's release from Europe. It took many months, and Diaghilev was obliged to start the tour in America a couple of months before Nijinsky could join them.

In the meantime, Nijinsky's roles in *Faune, Petrushka, Scheherazade* and *L'Oiseau de feu* were performed by Massine. The tour got off to a slow start – Nijinsky and Karsavina were missed and some adjustments had to be made to the programme for American audiences, who were both less sophisticated and less tolerant than in Europe. *Scheherazade* and *Faune* were both met with moral indignation. *Scheherazade* was denounced as politically incorrect and had to be cancelled in the South because of the heroine taking a black lover. The orgasmic finale at the end of *Faune* was subject to a complaint by the Catholic Theatre Board, culminating in the drama of a hearing in New York and a resulting toning down of the sexual innuendoes.

On their way through Europe, the Nijinskys visited the Stravinskys, who had been cut off from their Russian estate by the war and were living on a low income in Switzerland, near Lausanne. It was a blissful experience for Nijinsky to be able to speak to a fellow artist in his own language again. He felt sufficiently buoyed by bonhomie to ask his host if Kyra could stay with the Stravinsky family of seven children while they were in America. Stravinsky turned him down flat: he said he did not want the responsibility.

> *Stravinsky said he was sorry, but he could not take the child as he was afraid of infection and did not want to be responsible for my little Kyra's death ... Stravinsky is a dry man... He is a good composer of music but he does not write about life.*

Nijinsky wrote: "(Diaghilev) cannot live without Nijinsky and Stravinsky cannot live without Diaghilev." But it was not apparent at the time: Stravinsky was devastated not to be included in the American tour as Diaghilev had promised. He asked Nijinsky to demand that he join the tour. They composed a telegram to Diaghilev together, but Romola took it upon herself to tone it down in her translation, and there was no response.

AMERICA

The Nijinskys boarded the SS *Rochambeau* in France and, on 7 April 1916, arrived in New York. This time they were met at the dock by Diaghilev, in a gesture of reconciliation. He needed to make sure that there were no hitches to Nijinsky's participation and sincerely wanted to improve his relationship with Nijinsky's wife. Diaghilev could not afford any complications and was dependent on the success of this first North American tour. It had forced him to overcome his fear of travelling on the water, although he spent the entire voyage sitting on deck wearing his coat and tie, wearing two lifebelts and drinking whisky.

Safely recovered on land, he kissed his former lover on both cheeks and handed Romola a bunch of flowers. He was a bit nonplussed when they handed him the baby. True to form, Diaghilev had arrived with a horde of reporters, who had been talked into expecting Nijinsky's star quality to lift the tour. The Nijinskys were enthralled by their first sighting of Manhattan and, to the delight of the reporters, Nijinsky began to jump.

After the deprivation of the last two years, the affluence of America and the lavishness of the welcome were overwhelming. The God of Dance was about to unleash his power on stage again. For Nijinsky, it was as if he had never been away – the last two years seemed merely a nightmare. His enthusiasm for the city was reflected in his dancing and the choreography he was working on for *Till*, but no-one had bargained for the ugly intervention of money. The Ballets

Russes had already been on tour in North America for two months, and Nijinsky was scheduled to make his first appearance several days after his arrival. On the way to America, the Nijinskys had received word that they had won a court case in London demanding half a million francs in unpaid salary due to his unorthodox arrangement with Diaghilev, but Romola had been advised that they could have trouble recovering it, as Nijinsky was not a resident of any country.

Romola encouraged Nijinsky to refuse to perform until after he had been paid. Romola was a strong personality from a pampered background who loved her husband but saw him as an ornament and, like Diaghilev, believed she could "mould" him. Nijinsky's compliant personality made him increasingly reliant on her, but he was uncomfortable with her aggressive business demands. His sensitive soul was stifled by such behaviour. The chairman of the Metropolitan Opera House, Otto Kahn, was briefed about the financial hitch and the delicate situation had to be negotiated by solicitors before Nijinsky could perform again for the Ballets Russes.

The case was settled in their favour within a few days, but it was a bad beginning to the tour – the financial wrangles had created bad blood, and there were misunderstandings and negative mutterings within the company.

Nijinsky finally gave his first performance in two years at the Metropolitan Opera House on 12 April. He was pronounced sensational by most critics although, in some opinions, perceived as effeminate in *Spectre* and "amusing" in *Narcisse.* Nevertheless, he was credited with re-energising the company as hoped and was bombarded like a pop star of today. His underwear was stolen by fans and he and Romola were thrust on the celebrity bandwagon, entertained by the rich and famous and invited to open exhibitions and attend functions. Nijinsky was asked by Mrs William Vanderbilt to perform at a fundraising evening for the flood victims of Venice. He flatly refused to perform *Faune* – which Massine had been performing and the choreography tampered with – because there was no time to restore it to his original version.

American critic Carl Van Vetchen waxed lyrical about the qualities that set Nijinsky apart from the rest of the dancers:

> *I have never been able to discover the flaws in the art of this young man ... but it is a different matter to give the spirit of Nijinsky, to describe his art on paper ... Future generations must take our word for his greatness. His dancing has the unbroken quality of music, the balance of great painting, the meaning of fine literature and the emotion in all these arts.*

The three-week tour ended in such success that a second, more extensive, tour was proposed for the autumn. The Metropolitan Opera House, as producers, were so impressed by the company that they embarked on plans for a forty-week fifty-three-city tour across the United States and Canada with the intention of culturally educating the American public. There was some contention with Diaghilev, which caused Otto Kahn to support the proposal that Nijinsky both dance and direct the company without Diaghilev and the *regisseur* Grigoriev.

It was an extraordinary idea, considering the disaster of the London experience, but a risk that Diaghilev was forced to accept, as he had little chance of any other engagements in Europe during the war. It was a very ambitious tour that Otto Kahn was said to "have risked his shirt on", costing half a million dollars and involving a hundred and fifty people. The orchestra travelled with the company on a special train, and special cars were made to accommodate the scenery.

In a total turnaround from his position of a few months earlier as a prisoner of war, Nijinsky was once again at the helm of a company – despite his discomfort in the role.

In his forced exclusion from the tour, Diaghilev took up the invitation of royal balletomane King Alfonso XIII to form a second, experimental company in Spain with Massine. It was the forerunner of the strategy of many 21st-century companies in splitting their operation: the main company touring America was to be the moneymaking troupe and the Spanish section a vehicle for developing new works.

TILL EULENSPIEGEL

In the interim between tours, Nijinsky took his wife and daughter to holiday in New England, where he finally learnt to play the game of tennis that he had portrayed in *Jeux* and worked on the choreography for his new ballets. Realising it was unrealistic to produce two new works – *Mephisto Valse* (based on Liszt's *Mephisto*-Walzer) with its forty-five characters was far too ambitious a project to produce in such a short period – Nijinsky made the decision to concentrate on *Till Eulenspiegel.* Much of his time on the project was spent liaising with Robert Edmond Jones, a young American designer whom he had commissioned to create a modern concept of the Middle Ages.

When they were researching the origin of *Till* for their reconstruction for the Paris Opera in 1995, the *répétiteurs* of the ballet, Millicent Hodson and Kenneth Archer, came across an account of the collaboration between Nijinsky and Jones written by their interpreter, musician Ernest de Weerth:

> *Jones spread his very effective sketches over the floor. Nijinsky stood studying the paintings for some time. He turned to me: "Pencil. Two Pencils. One black. One red." To my surprise (and the unquestionable consternation of poor Bobby Jones) Nijinsky dropped onto the floor and began drawing lines on the actual sketch of the stage set. With the black pencil he threw all the houses and towers out of gear, making them crooked and leaning and toppling in every*

> *direction. Just as a naughty child might act, he looked up thoroughly satisfied with his mischief and grinned from ear to ear. "Till see everything distorted!" He explained.*
>
> *As an artist himself, Nijinsky urged Jones to use a more daring line in costuming and kept repeating: "Till see everything exaggerated. You understand, Bobby? Ernest? You tell Bobby. He not understand. He angry. Paintings lovely. Must be more extravagant."*

Nijinsky praised Jones to the press as "a greater colour artist than Bakst," who had captured the medieval fantasy in his striking costumes and décor but, by an appalling miscalculation, the sets were too short. They had to be lengthened at the bottom, so Nijinsky kept the lower part in shadow during performances. Carl Van Vechten described the sets and costumes as "decidedly diverting. Over a deep spreading background of ultramarine, the crazy turrets of medieval castles leaned dizzily to and fro. The costumes were exaggerations of the exaggerated fashions of the Middle Ages. Mr Jones added feet of stature to the already elongated peaked headdresses of the period. The trains of the velvet robes which might have extended three yards were allowed to trail the full length of the Metropolitan stage".

It was an inspirational experience for the young Jones. Nijinsky wrote in his diary that Jones was nervous and worried, but Jones was overwhelmed by Nijinsky's genius. Years later, he recalled his first meeting with "an extremely pretty woman, fashionably dressed in black and a small, somewhat stocky man, walking with delicate birdlike steps. He is very nervous. His eyes are troubled. He looks eager, anxious, excessively intelligent. He seems tired, bored, excited all at once. I observe that he has a disturbing habit of picking at the flesh on the side of his thumbs until they bleed. Through all my memories of this great artist runs the recurring image of those raw red thumbs. He broods and dreams, goes away into a reverie, returns again. At intervals his face lights up with a brief, dazzling smile. His manner is simple, ingratiating, so direct as to be almost humble. I like him at once.... I see no trace of the legendary exotic. Here is only the straightforward approach of the newly appointed maestro of the Russian Ballet who has an idea and wants it carried out".

He writes of Nijinsky's "extraordinary nervous energy, astonishing drive, a mental engine too high powered, racing to its final breakdown … Too eager, too brilliant, a quickening of the nerves, a merciless creative urge".

The Nijinskys' role in society during the tour was much more Romola's metier than her husband's: it was the life she had aspired to as the wife of the famous Nijinsky, to which she was accustomed as the daughter of the great Emilia Markus. Romola thrived on society, and the invitations poured in from the cities they toured. She was in her element – revelling in the social opportunities and her love of the luxuries of life.

Nijinsky and Romola had little in common: as with Nijinsky and Diaghilev, their personalities and backgrounds were totally opposed. Nijinsky endured the essential social occasions but spent all other spare moments developing his choreography. He had a heavy commitment and a tight schedule.

The tour was an enormous undertaking: during the forty weeks, three of which were in New York, the company performed in about fifty cities. Nijinsky was charged with the responsibility of staging a whole repertoire of ballets in a variety of theatres, the majority of which were not designed for ballet. He had to manage the mind-blowing logistics of moving the company, sets, props, costumes and equipment around the country and raising the curtain on a professional show every night. He had to deal with the personal problems of the group, save some nervous energy to perform himself as the star attraction and, on top of that, produce a complex new ballet. He was contracted to perform five nights a week and sometimes performed more than that. It was a Herculean task for anyone, let alone someone of Nijinsky's inexperience and introverted sensitive nature. He was running on highly charged nervous energy.

The Ballets Russes spent Christmas in the Californian desert travelling from Colorado to Los Angeles. They went to Salt Lake City and met native Indians and Mormons; in New Orleans, they were prevented from performing *Scheherazade* because of the political impropriety of a black slave making love to a white woman. In the work. During the season in Washington state, a journalist remarked that she wanted "to see the fellow Nijinsky dance, but why doesn't he get a real job?"

Nijinsky's family relate that the first thing Nijinsky always did on arrival in a city was visit the theatre. He was elated in Kansas to find it to be the only theatre in the whole of America with a raked stage like the Russian theatres.

Philosophically, Nijinsky had become an increasingly dedicated follower of Tolstoy and the influence was evident in his choreography for *Till Eulenspiegel.* The name *Eulenspiegel,* meaning "owl's mirror", was chosen for the owl, representing a symbol of wisdom and the mirror reflecting people to themselves.

The story is set in the German town of Brunswick during the Middle Ages. Nijinsky danced the main role of the rebel prankster Till, who is mischievous and mocking of individuals and society in general – a character similar to Shakespeare's Puck of *A Midsummer Night's Dream.* Till runs amok in the marketplace and is finally hanged, but his spirit lives on. The Five Urchins mock different groups of society in the manner of a Greek chorus. The ballet is packed with dancing, each gesture carefully choreographed to express a separate thought, and Till's solo is a manifesto of freedom – showing the people that they can free themselves.

In the manner of all contemporary choreographers, Nijinsky reflected his own reaction to the themes of the world around him: in *Till,* he depicted the world of 1916 with war in Europe and unrest erupting in Russia. He wrote in his diary, "I made this comic ballet because I felt the war. Everyone was sick of the war and therefore people wanted to be cheered up. I showed *Till* in all its beauty. I showed that it was the German people."

On the first day of rehearsal, Nijinsky was confronted with a new obstacle. The dancers went on strike refusing, as Russians, to dance to German music while their countries were at war. Striking was a new phenomenon to the Russian artists, and the Metropolitan management was forced to warn them that they were legally contracted to perform to all the music: if they did not fulfil their contracts, they were liable to be deported.

Till was a hugely ambitious work: the eighteen-minute ballet for more than twenty dancers, with twenty solo parts, had to be totally produced in just three weeks. Nijinsky's nervous energy reached manic proportions. Jones relished his days as if he was in a dream, wondering, "Can life, be so rich, so splendid, so passionate?"

The bubble burst when Jones produced his completed set for *Till* on stage. In the middle of the frenetic rehearsal period, he caught the full brunt of Nijinsky's rage. The set was too shallow, with not enough space for the dancers and not high enough to give the effect of crazy exaggeration that Nijinsky had visualised. That afternoon, Nijinsky slipped when he was jumping up on stage to correct one of the dancers. He fainted, sprained his ankle and was ordered to rest completely for six weeks. "Your scenery is so bad," the dancers told Jones, "that when the maestro saw it, he fell down."

Nijinsky was under enormous strain but had no choice but to continue conducting operations as best he could in his incapacitated state and postpone dancing for a couple of weeks. Luckily, he had completed all but the final brief scene, which he asked the dancers to improvise. Jones solved the problem of room by repositioning the set further back on stage and elongating it by adding an extra 10-foot-high canvas to the base of the trees and houses of the represented town.

When the ballet finally premiered in New York on 23 October 1916, it was premature: it was ahead of its time, in concept and choreography, but rushed and unrefined. Nijinsky wrote in his diary, "I cooked it very well, but it was taken out of the oven too soon." Because of its complex groupings and individual diversifications for each dancer, it would have benefited from more rehearsal time.

Till was nevertheless heralded as Nijinsky's best ballet – the public loved Nijinsky's "comic" work. Nijinsky explained his intentions for the work to the critics before the premiere. It was both a departure for him in subject and genre: in the grim climate of the war-torn world, he had deliberately chosen to stage a comic work. The company was rewarded with dazzling ovations and reviews. It was a universal success with dancers, audiences and critics during its many performances on the tour.

Till is the zenith of Nijinsky's work: in contrast to his other ballets, the dancers enjoyed working on it and regarded it as his best work. And it is probably the only time he functioned completely as a creator in his own right without the external influence of Diaghilev, Bakst or any other artists. It is lamentable that it was never performed in Europe and was the only one of his ballets that Diaghilev did not see. Nijinsky was out of favour and, despite the glowing reviews, Diaghilev and his supporters disparaged the work.

Although *Till* sadly sank from trace with the general ballet public, Hodson and Archer consider it a milestone work, the forerunner of the genre of dance drama that has engaged choreographers since the 1970s:

> *The cascading apples have their present-day counterpart in Ian Spink's Bosendorfer Waltzes ... and in the apples, leaves, grass, carnations and mud of various pieces by Pina Basuch. Nijinsky in* Till *jumped a good half a century forward: for him, as for many artists now, the stage was not a void but a crossroads of colliding references.*

It was also hailed as the pinnacle of Nijinsky's own performing style: enhanced by his eccentric mime, it was virtuosity with a difference. Some critics declared *Till* the greatest spectacle of the Ballets Russes: "With *Faune and Petrushka,* it forms a trio of mimic masterpieces and for scenic effects, is way ahead of anything the ballet has done." It was that triple bill that Hodson and Archer contributed to the Paris Opera. Their reconstruction of *Till* premiered in 1995 in a programme with their reconstruction of Nijinsky's other works *Sacre* and Fokine's *Petrushka.*

HT Parker of the *Boston Transcript* wrote in his review:

> *It is the handiwork of an intellect, invention and fancy that shows Mr Nijinsky more than the master dancer of his time; that offers a new and fruitful field to mimodrama:*

> *that confirms the distinction that marks the Russian ballet as one of the driving artistic forces of our time.*

Jones reminisced:

> *How shall I tell of this long-forgotten ballet, so fresh, so natural, so innocent, that it flashed and vanished like a forgotten dream? No critic, with the exception of HT Parker, seems to be able to appreciate it in its true relation to the other works in the Diaghilev repertoire. It was too original in its conception, too novel, too seldom performed … But without question it showed Nijinsky at the height of his creative power and I believe it to be one of the few genuine masterpieces – I use that word deliberately, in the entire recorded history of ballet.*

He dwells on "the great artist who taught me so much", and his "strange, magical, shattering experience … which gave him a heightened and broadened sense of life".

The Nijinsky association was continued for Jones by his later work with Nicolas Roerich, the conceptualiser/designer of *Sacre,* at the Master Institute of United Arts, of the Roerich Museum in New York during the 1930s.

DISCIPLE

Having developed his choreographic vision so dramatically, Nijinsky was rapidly becoming more dissatisfied with the endless repetitions of the Fokine ballets. He had moved far from what he saw as the affectations of the Romantic style. He was a deep thinker whose views were coloured by his growing belief in the Tolstoyan way of life and rejection of middle-class values. Nijinsky was following Duncan, the first choreographer to portray ugliness and to approach modern dance spiritually – to take its main purpose as dealing with the deepest concerns of humanity.

One of the dancers on the tour was Dmitri Kostrovsky – a strange, quiet man who suffered from epilepsy. He and Nikolai Zverev were disciples of Tolstoy. Kostrovsky began following Nijinsky around and monopolising his time. Nijinsky found he related to Kostrovsky and Zverev's obsession with the Tolstoyan philosophy. Both he and Bronislava had been given Tolstoy's works as prizes at the Imperial School and were familiar with his themes.

The three Russians spent hours talking together in their own language, often well into the night. Romola felt excluded – she did not speak their language and could not relate to their philosophy; it was totally opposed to her own emphasis on the finer material things of life. She became very agitated when Nijinsky began refusing to take part in social functions, started dressing in a Russian peasant shirt instead of a shirt and tie and insisting on vegetarianism for all of them, including little Kyra; he talked about practising celibacy and taking his wife and daughter to live a peasant's life in Russia.

Romola watched Kostrovsky's "fanatical" influence spread throughout the company. He lectured everyone on his beliefs. She became more alarmed when she thought it was beginning to have a bearing on Nijinsky's artistic judgement. Kostrovsky persuaded him that, as all men were equal, the artists should share their roles. The upshot was that Zverev performed Nijinsky's role of the Golden Slave in *Scheherazade* and the Spirit of the Rose in *Spectre.* Nijinsky ended up performing Cecchetti's role of the Eunuch on an occasion when the maestro was sick, but the most disturbing aspect was that it was all unannounced – the audience was under the impression they were seeing none other than Nijinsky or Cecchetti.

Because of her husband's commitment to his artistic work, Romola was forced to take on the role of assistant in non-artistic matters. One day, she received a note from a young Italian called Rodolfo Guglielmi begging to see Nijinsky and claiming it to be a matter of life and death. When Romola agreed to meet, the young man threw himself on his knees, pleading for her help. He had arrived from Sicily not long before and was desperately trying to get into film. To secure a particular role, he had lied about his experience and claimed that he was a professional dancer – a pupil of the great Nijinsky. Romola assured the traumatised young man that she would discuss the situation with her husband. The result was that Nijinsky generously gave the man time out of his busy schedule to show him some steps and movements. Whether or not it was the endorsement the young man was seeking, he later won fame as Julio in the film *Four Horsemen of the Apocalypse* and became a legend in his own right under the name of Rudolph Valentino.

Nijinsky's intolerance for the social side of the tour, the civic receptions and ancillary functions caused him to overreact on one occasion in Tulsa, Oklahoma. On arrival in the city, he swapped roles with the concertmaster, who was rather fat. The concertmaster/Nijinsky was photographed for a local paper, and it gave the local people a shock to see such a rotund star.

During the tour, Nijinsky experienced another setback: he received another summons for Russian military service. Ironically, it was the justification that he had been waiting for to return to his home country. He was yearning for Russia, which he had not visited for five years (since leaving with the Ballets Russes in 1911) and his family there were confident that he could convince the authorities that he was exempt from service. However, he was bound by his contract to the Metropolitan Opera House, which had only managed to obtain his release from Austria on the condition that he stay in neutral countries during the war and not take up arms against any of the powers.

It was a flashpoint for Nijinsky – he broke the tour to travel to Washington for discussions with the Russian embassy but was forced to accept the fact that he would have to continue the season as scheduled.

To his credit, Nijinsky encouraged less-experienced dancers of the *corps de ballet* to prepare for their future by learning the principal roles and acting as understudies. Later on the tour, he met Charles Chaplin in Hollywood and found him to be a kindred soul from the related world of film. Both men lived their lives wearing masks and transforming into multiple identities onstage. Offstage, they both retreated within themselves. Chaplin came backstage at the interval and was introduced to the company by Nijinsky, who enjoyed the meeting so much that the interval lasted twice as long as usual. Chaplin was just as captivated by Nijinsky and, in turn, invited him to visit the studio where he was filming *The Cure.* He said:

> *I have seen few geniuses in the world and Nijinsky was one of them. He was hypnotic, godlike, his somberness suggesting moods of other worlds: every movement was poetry, every leap a flight into strange fancy.*

He was becoming seriously committed to the Tolstoy philosophy. Romola was becoming desperate, as she felt Nijinsky drifting away from her. She thought him mesmerised by the two disciples Kostrovksy and Zvevrev, but he was strangely gloomy and meditative in their company. He was now obsessed with the Tolstoyan edict, which he believed touched the core of being. The philosophy embraced feelings deep within him of humanitarian values – for the government of love, truth and beauty.

Romola simply could not reconcile the idea of Nijinsky giving up his theatrical life to become a peasant farmer in Russia. She believed he was becoming physically weakened by his vegetarianism, which verged on veganism and did not even allow him to eat eggs. She was locked in a constant tussle with the Tolstoyans for her husband's attention. Romola felt that they had jeopardised his commitment to her. Her patience finally ran out. Romola hatched a bizarre plan of trying to "cure" Nijinsky. She took off for New York, telling him if he really wanted to live the life of Tolstoy, she would take Kyra and return to Europe – desperately hoping that her action would shock him into coming to his senses. Nijinsky could not function independently and could certainly not manage the tour without Romola's help. He had far too much to deal with: no 21st-century company would have their principal artist running the company without the support of a manager or rehearsal director.

By the time the Ballets Russes reached New York six weeks later, Romola was relieved to see that her plan appeared to have worked – her husband had rejected his peasant shirts and was overjoyed to see his family. He was dressing normally again, eating meat and appeared to have put away his plans for peasant life.

The long tour, which had started in mid-October, finally ended on 14 February 1917 with a performance in Albany, New York.

SPAIN

Nijinsky had little option but to accept Diaghilev's invitation to perform with the second company in Madrid and take part in a second tour to South America. He was bound by the terms of his contract, which stipulated that, as an alien, he could only dance in a neutral country. America was about to enter the war, and Nijinsky could not join the company tour to Italy, but was eligible for Spain, which was neutral.

The Ballets Russes opened in Madrid on 2 June 1917, with Nijinsky dancing *Scheherazade, Carnaval, Spectre* and *Faune.* The king and queen attended almost every night and many of the rehearsals. The king was rumoured to be in love with the beautiful Tchernicheva (Grigoriev's wife), and his cousin – the Duchess of Durcal, another of the Ballets Russes major supporters in Spain – had announced she was madly in love with Nijinsky. Oddly, Romola encouraged this liaison. Nijinsky was happy during this period: he was reconciled to a certain degree with Diaghilev, working creatively again and admired Massine – it was not in his nature to bear malice. He was fascinated by Massine's choreography in *Les Femmes de bonne humeur;* he wanted to help him and offered to dance in his works.

In contrast to the austerity of the Tolstoyan period, Nijinsky and Romola were thrust into Spanish society. They were back in Diaghilev's camp and had no chance of refusing his invitations to soirees and dinners. Romola writes of meeting Picasso:

> *He was very little known at the time. He was reticent and very Spanish looking and when he began to explain anything, he became full of excitement and used to draw on the tablecloth, the menu cards, and on the top of Sergei Pavlovich's walking stick.*

Nevertheless, Romola was aware that the "Tolstoyan threat", as she saw it, was not completely dead. Her encouragement of the Duchess's advances toward her husband was part of an overall scheme to throw him further off the Tolstoyan way of life. Romola perversely thrust them together and pronounced herself pleased when Nijinsky returned one night and mournfully told her, "*Femmka*, I am sorry for what I did. It was unfair to her, as I am not in love, and the added experience which you perhaps wanted me to have is unworthy of us."

Romola was becoming increasingly apprehensive about the forthcoming South American tour. She was worried about the risk of Nijinsky falling into his monk-like state again by spending long periods with Kostrovsky and Zverev. She used all her wiles to persuade him not to go. Eventually, she succeeded; Nijinsky acquiesced and agreed to withdraw from the tour. But his relationship with Diaghilev had sunk to a basic business level and, when Nijinsky told him of his decision, Diaghilev invoked the letter of the law. He told Nijinsky bluntly that he had no choice – that his cable agreeing in principle to the tour was a valid contract. He said he would force him to go. But Nijinsky retaliated that he had only agreed to discuss the tour when he reached Spain. His excuse of needing a rest was rather inept considering he had just had a two-month holiday between America and Spain and was only performing one or two ballets on the sixteen nights of the Spanish season. Diaghilev's tough stance infuriated Nijinsky – he was finally fed up with the years of Diaghilev's dominance and with that, told him he was finished with the Ballets Russes.

Nijinsky and Romola prepared to leave Barcelona, but as they were about to board their train, they were apprehended and arrested by the police. Romola, the major source of information on this period, writes how the police informed them that Diaghilev had asked them to prevent Nijinsky from breaking his contract. If he did not perform that night, he would be put in jail. Romola immediately put her networks into play. She contacted the Duc de Duval:

> *Within an hour an order arrived from Madrid for our immediate release and Señor Cambo, the eminent Spanish lawyer, arrived to take up our case with Diaghilev. The Barcelona authorities now realised that they had made a dreadful blunder, and were full of excuses. It was too late to catch the train, so we returned to the hotel where the Theatre director was awaiting us. The director cried at once: "The public is disappointed, they are returning their tickets by the hundreds. It's you they want to see dance. I am ruined because I have to pay Diaghilev whatever happens, and now I have not made a peso. My last season was a failure too."*

With that, Nijinsky said he would dance that night for the director's sake. The next day, the Nijinskys discussed the situation with Cambo. To their dismay, they discovered that Spain was the only country in which a cable was a legally binding contract and Nijinsky would have to go to South America. On Romola's insistence, Cambo drew up a contract demanding the same salary Nijinsky had received in North America, based on a form originated by the Austrian 19th-century ballerina Fanny Elssler after she had been cheated many times by dishonest impresarios. The contract stipulated that Nijinsky be paid in gold dollars an hour before each performance and if it was not honoured, it would become null and void.

It was a funereal ending to their Spanish sojourn and a sadly symbolic parting of the ways: Diaghilev and Massine and the sixteen-dancer company stayed in Europe while the Nijinskys sent Kyra to a school in Switzerland and set sail for South America. The rift between Diaghilev and Nijinsky was almost complete: Diaghilev was at the end of his tolerance with Nijinsky. The trouble with the police had severed his confidence in Nijinsky's ability to continue with the company. He had seen his first protégé perform for the last time and his focus was on a future with Massine.

Nijinsky was loyal and trusting by nature and revered Diaghilev's professional skills, but it was the death of the last shred of personal esteem he may have held for his former lover.

SOUTH AMERICA

On the ship, the Nijinskys met George de Cuevas, whom Romola described as: "A typical gigolo, extremely well bred and dressed." He was a Chilean who later inherited a Spanish title and formed a ballet company in Monte Carlo, for which Bronislava mounted *The Sleeping Beauty* in 1960.

It had been an extremely stressful period. Nijinsky was emotionally exhausted, drained by the wrangling between the two major players in his life. The tension was anathema to his simple, sensitive soul. The drama deepened when Kostrovsky suffered an epileptic fit during the tour. He was diagnosed as incurably insane and sent back to Russia. Had the diagnosis happened earlier, he would not have had time to interfere with Nijinsky's thinking to the same degree, and the scenario might have been vastly different.

The incident over the contract had created a bad relationship with Grigoriev, who was back in charge of the company. He considered the Nijinskys to be enemies of Diaghilev and treated them coldly. His attitude created a bad climate within the company, and most of the other dancers were cool towards Nijinsky. Nijinsky felt isolated. He began to feel persecuted in the uneasy environment, and the company became increasingly alarmed by his disturbed behaviour. The situation spawned a ludicrous incident of Nijinsky blocking the performance of *Faune*. The audience waited restlessly in their seats while the presenter tried to reason with the police over an injunction brought by Nijinsky, the creator of *Faune*, to prevent its performance, as the company did not own the rights and had not negotiated any agreement for its performance during the tour; while Nijinsky the performer paced up and down in the wings as he waited to go on stage according to his contract. The crunch came when the impresario was asked if he had anything in writing to prove that they had the author's permission to perform the work. As formal contracts were never a priority for Diaghilev and none existed, the ballet could not be performed.

Despite the internal tension within the company, Nijinsky's public persona was highly respected on the tour, and he won many friends and supporters. In Rio de Janeiro, the scene of their engagement four years before, the Nijinskys were entertained royally by the Russian and American ambassadors. The French ambassador was the poet Paul Claudel, who was captivated by Nijinsky's dancing and wrote:

> *He moved like a tiger. There was no change of inert weight from one pose to another. His spring came from a buoyant partnership of muscular and nervous energy, like a bird on the wing. There was not a gesture, be it ever so slight (as for example when he turned his chin towards us, and the small head revolved on its long neck) which he did not accomplish magnificently, with a vivacity at once fierce and gentle with an astonishing authority. Even in repose he seemed imperceptibly to be dancing, like those luxuriously sprung carriages which used to be called "huit-ressorts".*

Claudel was working on two ballets – *L'homme et son desir* and *La Creation du Monde* – with the composer Darius Milhaud (his secretary at the post, who became a member of a group of avant-garde French musicians known as *Le Six* along with Durey, Honegegger, Talliferre, Aurie and Poulenc – Misia Sert introduced these last two, and Milhaud, to Diaghilev). They asked Nijinsky to create the choreography for them, and he gladly accepted, but the project was destined to be among the casualties of his future.

Nijinsky and Romola also became very friendly with the composer Oswald d'Estrade-Guerra and his pianist wife Niniha.

Nijinsky often spoke to them proudly about his baby daughter Kyra and showed them the photo of her he always carried. In talking about ballet, Nijinsky told d'Estrade-Guerra that his sister Bronislava and Karsavina were the world's two greatest contemporary dancers. He also confided in him that he intended to leave the company after the tour. When d'Estrade-Guerra later heard the tragic news of Nijinsky's breakdown, he could not believe it. He had found Nijinsky a highly intelligent, lucid and unpretentious man. Any unusual factors he put down to his being a highly strung artist and a Slav. He said Nijinsky had an "intelligent childlike, natural side to his character, without the slightest pretension. When I heard that he had gone insane, I was unable to believe it. Nothing in our meetings in Brazil could have led me to foresee that".

In Buenos Aries, the Nijinskys were entertained by the priest who married them; they ran into Pavlova, who was also dancing in the city and George de Cuevas, whom they had met on board the ship.

On the professional front, the situation within the company was deteriorating further. There were a number of small incidents that fed Nijinsky's persecution mania: he stepped on a rusty nail on stage, he narrowly missed an iron weight falling by leaping out of the way and the puppets' booth in *Petrushka* collapsed during a performance. His mental stability was beginning to fray. He was tormented by thoughts of being surrounded by spies and believed everything that went wrong to be a plot of Grigoriev's. His behaviour was becoming very uneven – intense outbursts followed by periods of introspection. After he finished dancing, Nijinsky often continued to leap and gesticulate for some time afterwards, which was weird and worrying to observe. Romola was convinced that the string of incidents was a deliberate plot to force Nijinsky to pay the penalty of 20,000 dollars if he broke his contract. She hired a detective to watch over him at the theatre.

One day, Nijinsky declared he had forgotten his part in *Narcisse;* on another occasion, he had a manic conviction that Grigoriev would give the wrong signal and open the trap on stage. There was another crisis when Nijinsky would not settle into his starting position for *L'Apres-midi d'un faune.* Everyone was in place waiting for the curtain to go up, but Nijinsky was tearing wildly around the stage, refusing to listen to reason. In desperation, the stage manager gave the order to raise the curtain. For a second, the audience was confronted with a dazed Nijinsky as he rushed offstage. The curtain was lowered again and he climbed into position on the hill and performed the ballet.

The tour gradually wound to a close and, on 26 September 1917, Nijinsky performed for the last time with the Ballets Russes. Fittingly, it was with performances of his legendary *Le Spectre de la rose* and *Petrushka.*

On the way home, Nijinsky arranged to support the Red Cross by performing at a fundraising gala matinee for wounded soldiers in Montevideo, Uruguay. He was keen to support such a worthy cause but restricted in his choice of repertoire as most of his sets and costumes were on their way back to Europe with the company freight. He performed *Ministrels* by Debussy. The rest of the programme included a recital by pianist Arthur Rubenstein and some opera arias.

Romola could not grasp much of what motivated Nijinsky but understood his sense of loss of position in the company and his disillusion. The public saw an extraordinary performer at the height of his powers, but something was now missing for Nijinsky. He was no longer satisfied with just performing and was brimming with ideas for new choreography. He wrote in his diary: "I do not want to dance the way I used to, because those dances are death." But the Ballets Russes no longer offered him the unlimited opportunities it had previously, now that Diaghilev was devoted to encouraging the choreography of Massine. Romola defiantly supported Nijinsky's decision to leave the Ballet Russes.

DETERIORATION AND CREATION

Nijinsky had become obsessed with two themes: the war and the insidiousness of the Diaghilev clique. He was looking for a means of escape from them both and a way to develop new works. His mind was also dwelling on his long-fostered dream of opening a school to train dancers in the individual style of his new work. At the time, the only training was classical. In the meantime, he was looking forward to reunion with Kyra and a rest.

The Nijinskys returned to Europe and settled in Switzerland, taking a house called Villa Guardamunt at St Moritz – the first home of their own. Kyra was now four years old and as devoted to her father as he was to her. Romola wrote:

> *It almost felt as though they were one person split apart and constantly wishing to be reunited. They were both so fundamentally Russian. Sometimes I felt as if I was intruding on them.*

Nijinsky did his *barre* – his ballet exercises – for two hours every morning on the balcony on the ground floor with Kyra watching his every move laughing and clapping her hands, calling out to "Tatakaboy", as she called him. Nijinsky loved the snow and drove the family in a sleigh on excursions exploring the glaciers and lakes of the area and either picnicking or stopping at a roadside café. He was working seriously in his studio, engrossed in developing his most pressing ideas. Much of the time was spent developing his new system of dance notation – a complex system of musical notes augmented with symbols and words, based on the circle. He painstakingly transcribed all of *Faune,* but the system was too complicated for the other ballets. He ironically observed that "the notation of *Faune* took about two months to notate and ten minutes to perform". He was obsessed with the shape of the circle and told Romola that it was "the complete, the perfect movement. Everything is based on it – life and most certainly our art. It is the perfect line". He talked of even building a round theatre.

The circle was the basis of the ballet he was working on: a choreographic poem of a youth seeking truth through life, first as a pupil open to all artistic suggestions to all the beauty that life and love can offer then to love for his mate, who finally carries him off. Nijinsky set the ballet in the High Renaissance, with the youth as a painter and his master one of the greatest artists of the period, a universal genius, as he himself perceived Diaghilev. Nijinsky worked out the design for the scenery and costumes himself, making them correct in the smallest detail to the period, in blue, red and gold, Raphaelistic style. In keeping with his obsession with the circle, the scenery was designed in a curve, and even the proscenium opening was round.

He was also working on two scenes to Debussy's music *Chansons de Bilitis* based on the same choreographic laws as *Faune.* He read books and pondered more ballets – and gloried in spending the rest of his time occupied with domesticity, chopping wood and pottering around the kitchen. Offers to dance poured in from impresarios around the world, but Nijinsky was deeply affected by the war and said he could not dance until it was over.

One of his ideas was named *Les Papillons de nuit,* which would show "the beauty and destructive quality of love" through sex, though dance critics argue that Nijinsky operated on a sensual basis, not sexual, even in his depiction of *Faune.* He asked Romola to assist him with the idea by letting him hypnotise her.

She describes how when she obliged, "I began to dance, strangely fascinated by Vaslav's oblique eyes, which he almost closed as if he wanted to shut out of himself everything except my dancing. When I finished he said that I danced with a wonderful technique all the different parts of his newly composed ballet."

When Romola asked how he would complete the ballet, Nijinsky fell into one of his long silences. He was alternatively meditative and restless. Starved of the stage, Nijinsky turned to other means of expression – painting, drawing and writing – which he did not find easy, in a desperate bid to find an outlet for his overflowing mind.

He was constantly developing new ideas, inventing a fountain pen for his rush of writing, a windscreen wiper, a "bridge railway" across the sea and various other projects. His mind was in constant turmoil, churning with ideas.

His hours spent drawing and painting produced abstract work – frequently on circular themes, often in the form of strange circular portraits. Romola was disturbed by the bizarre faces with eyes peering from every corner, red and black, like a blood-stained mortuary cover; fanciful butterflies with faces like his own and big spiders with faces similar to that of Diaghilev. One of Nijinsky's recurring themes was of frightening insane eyes in the middle of spider-web-like forms. He was reading Maeterlinck's *La Mort* and Nietzsche's *Ecce Homo.*

During this extended time offstage, the Nijinskys were leading an isolated life in their villa in the Swiss mountains. There were few callers and their main physical activities were walks. Nijinsky frenetically flung himself into winter sports: he took up skiing and drove Romola and Kyra down the slopes in a sled at a frenzied pace that matched the machinations of his mind. After his previous action-packed existence of constantly travelling and the elation of performing, Nijinsky frequently behaved like a caged animal. There was no room in the small house for him to move and practise properly. Although he was finding new creative outlets, he was frustrated without an audience.

The introspective life reinforced Nijinsky's belief in the Tolstoyan philosophy. He became entrenched in that lifestyle, returning to vegetarianism and refusing food with any trace of meat. His behaviour was becoming increasingly irrational; his communication with Romola and the rest of the world was deteriorating – he was retreating more often into periods of silence and suffered from a lot of headaches. Romola became gradually aware that her husband was very depressed. He was slowly losing contact with reality and immersing himself in his own fantastic world. God had become implanted in his psyche. He began going for long walks around the village and surrounding hills wearing a heavy iron cross around his neck.

It was difficult to assess his exact mental state because of his moments of supreme lucidity. On one occasion, Nijinsky amazed a visiting Hungarian mathematician with his knowledge of mathematics.

Romola writes of outbursts of sudden violence. Without warning, one day Nijinsky suddenly attacked their maid, leaping at her and holding her by the throat until he was disturbed by Romola calling from another room. The maid fled and the tension rose. On another day, he pushed them both down the stairs.

It was a turning point in his mental health. Romola realised that she needed to seek help and consulted a local doctor, who studied Nijinsky under the pretext of a social situation. She was greatly relieved when the doctor's diagnosis was that her husband was suffering from hysteria due to overwork. They arranged for him to be supervised by a nurse masquerading as a masseur.

Their schemes did not escape Nijinsky. Strangely, he seemed to be aware of his deteriorating state and when he began later recording his inner turmoil, wrote that he did not want people to think he was a great writer, a great artist or a great man:

> *I am a simple man who has suffered a lot .... My sickness is that of the soul and not of the mind. I know what I need in order to become well again. My sickness is too great for me to be cured of it soon. I am a man and not God. I want to dance. I want to draw. I want to play the piano. I want to write poetry. I want to compose ballets. I want to love*

> *everyone. This is my aim in life. I am the whole world. I am the earth. I do not want to have property. I do not want to be rich. I want to love, love ... I want happiness for everyone. I shall be the happiest of men when I shall act and dance ... without monetary or any other kind of reward. I want love for people.*

Then he revealed that he had been acting. He told the visiting Duc and Duquesa de Ducal, "I am an artist; I have no troupe now, so ... for six weeks I played the part of a lunatic, and the whole village, my family, and even the physicians believed it. I have a male nurse to watch me, in the guise of a masseur." It was an avowal that was confirmed by the nurse/masseur, who told Romola that he considered Nijinsky completely sane.

LAST DANCE

Romola was delirious with relief at the reprieve, especially when Nijinsky announced that he wanted to give another dance performance. With the help of the doctor, she made arrangements for the performance to be a fundraising function for the Red Cross, held in the ballroom of the elegant Suvretta House hotel nearby on the afternoon of Sunday 19 July 1919. She booked pianist Bertha Glebar Asseo as his accompanist. Nijinsky liaised with the local dressmaker to organise his own costumes but refused to tell anyone what he was going to dance or ask Bertha to play.

On the day of the performance, Nijinsky entered the hall and announced to the audience of about two hundred people: "I will show you how we live, how we suffer, how we artists create." He then sat down on a chair facing them. Romola describes how they all sat there hypnotised during a long, awkward period of silence. She became more and more agitated – the situation seemed out of control. Eventually, the pianist started to play *Les Sylphides* and *Spectre*, in desperation, hoping that the familiar music would help him begin. It appeared to have no effect. When Romola approached and urged him to start dancing, Nijinsky angrily retorted: "Do not disturb me! I am not a machine. I will dance when I feel like it."

Mortified, Romola left the room and prepared to take her husband home, but when she returned, Nijinsky had begun dancing "gloriously, but frighteningly," to the music of Chopin. His unrehearsed movements came from deep within him and conveyed his nervous excitement. The performance was the culmination of many of the ideas and emotions of his brimming mind and soul. Stretching his arms sideways, he reached upwards as if praying, letting them drop noisily. The audience sat in uncomfortable silence, unprepared for such an unconventional performance. The tension was palpable. They were not used to stillness in choreography or such a naked outpouring. Nijinsky was pioneering another new choreographic phenomenon – he was finding yet another form of expressing his feelings. He recounts in his diary that he realised that the audience might want to be amused and suddenly changed to a merry dance; the audience relaxed and some laughed. Then his mood abruptly changed again. Romola describes the performance:

> *He took a few rolls of black and white velvet and made a big cross the length of the room. He stood at the head of it with open arms, a living cross himself. He began a sermon, telling of the horror of the war, of the millions of lost lives: "Now I will dance you the war, with its suffering, with its destruction, with its death. The war which you did not prevent and so you are also responsible for."*

He then began to move fast, leaping in his spectacular style, building to a wild crescendo. Romola wrote:

> *Vaslav's dancing was as brilliant, as wonderful as ever, but it was different. Sometimes it vaguely reminded me of that scene in Petrushka when the puppet tries to escape his fate. He seemed to fill the room with horror-stricken suffering humanity. It was tragic; his gestures were all monumental, and he entranced us so that we almost saw him floating over corpses. The public sat breathlessly horrified and so strangely fascinated. They seemed to be petrified. But we felt that Vaslav was like one of those overpowering creatures full of dominating strength, a tiger let out of the jungle, who in any moment could destroy us. And he was dancing, dancing on. Whirling through space,*

> *taking his audience away with him to war, to destruction, facing suffering and horror, struggling with his steel-like muscles, his agility, his lightning quickness, his ethereal being, to escape the inevitable end. It was the dance for life against death.*

Then, as suddenly as he had begun, Nijinsky stopped his tortured performance, put his hand on his heart and said, "This little horse is tired." He wrote in his diary:

> *The audience came to be amused. .... I danced frightening things. They were frightened of me and therefore thought that I wanted to kill them. I did not want to kill anyone. I loved everyone, but nobody loved me and therefore I became nervous. Then I began to play cheerful things. The audience cheered up...The audience too laughed in the dance. .... I danced badly; I kept falling on the floor when I did not have to. The audience did not care, because I danced beautifully. They understood my tricks and enjoyed themselves. I wanted to dance more, but God said to me: "Enough." I stopped .... In the carriage I told my wife that today was the day of my marriage with God.*

It was Nijinsky's last public performance; an astonishing experience for the audience and for Romola – it could not be further removed from the gay abandon of *Carnaval, Scheherazade* and *Le Spectre de la rose* of his recent past.

Nijinsky acted even more strangely at the reception afterwards, thinking a woman who complimented him was flirting with him, breaking into what he described as a "tart's dance" and falling on the floor. Romola was very distressed by his behaviour. As she was leaving, the pianist said to her, "It must be very, very difficult being married to a genius like Nijinsky."

SELF-REFLECTION

Nijinsky's behaviour became increasingly erratic during the next few weeks. It was during this time that began his diary. He stopped working on new ballets or drawings and focused on his journal. He was immersed in self-reflection, in recording his spiritual journey He wrote of his hallucinations using direct terms as if he were God. He found the need, after years of silence, to express his innermost thoughts in an outpouring of writing as if a race against time. In a frenetic six weeks, he recorded an analysis of his distorted mind in four red, leather-bound notebooks illustrated with musical staves and weird circular drawings.

Writing in a neat-pencilled hand, in deliberately small handwriting to economise on paper, he spilled it all out in a continuous narrative without the separation of paragraphs or subject matter in a mixture of Russian and some French. Nijinsky explained that he would prefer his handwriting to be photographed, rather than printed: "Handwriting is a beautiful thing and therefore it must be preserved. I want my handwriting to be photographed to explain my hand, because my hand is God's. I want to write in God's way and therefore I do not correct my writing."

He was consumed by the exercise. The diary charts the gradual disintegration of his unquiet mind from the horrors of the First World War, Diaghilev's cruel treatment of him after his marriage and the artistic pressures and frustrations of creativity. Yet it resonates with his belief in universal love and humanitarian edicts. His deep commitment to the beliefs of Tolstoy had threatened both his marriage and his dancing career. His intuitive performance and humanitarian views had prompted Isadora Duncan to propose to him in 1909 and again later, that they should have a child together. Just as Nijinsky's views of art heralded modernity, his views on living project forward to attitudes of today with his dislike of drugs, his pleas for vegetarianism, conservation and self-denial, and his belief in equality and concern for the poor. His passion for human rights could well have developed from his experience in St Petersburg on Bloody Sunday, 9 January 1905.

Nijinsky's intention was for the diaries to be published in two volumes: *On Life* and *On Death*. He was adamant that he wanted his books to be free, not "published for money".

In his dense prose, Nijinsky's disciples believe, lie simple messages for mankind. They believe Nijinsky to have been a true communicator and leader in the search for meaning in life, but much of his frustration could well be his failure to satisfactorily convey his messages. Even in his own medium of dance, his ideas were little understood. He wrote, "I am writing this book for the sake of its ideas and not for the sake of its handwriting," and, "I know many people will say that I write nonsense, but I say that everything I write has a deep meaning. I am a man with meaning." Also: "I feel before I see .... My mind is so developed that I understand people without words .... My thoughts proceed calmly and not abruptly."

The epilogue is signed:

God and Nijinsky.
Saint Moritz Dorf.
Villa Guardamunt.
27 February 1919.

FATE

The next part of Nijinsky's story was reliant on Romola's interpretation until psychiatrist Peter Ostwald researched Nijinsky's medical records and published his book *Vaslav Nijinsky: A Leap into Madness* (1991). His perceptive professional view offers an alternative interpretation of the story. It is invaluable in filling in the picture of Nijinsky's darkening years.

Few of the reasons for Nijinsky's conflicts were clear to those around him in St Moritz in 1919. The local doctor enlisted by Romola was now trying to psychoanalyse Nijinsky, observing him on a daily basis. The doctor's name has been deliberately undisclosed, although Nijinsky refers to him in his diary as Frenkel. He is a mysterious character in the story. He was the hotel doctor at a nearby resort who specialised in sports medicine, described in Ostwald's book as "a bohemian, musical and nature-loving man," handsome, ambitious, married, a few years older than Nijinsky, with a daughter the same age as Kyra. He was fascinated by the great dancer's case and also the woman who married him, whom he diagnosed as having her own psychological problems. Soon, Romola was looking to him for comfort and advice. There are suggestions that they had an affair. Ostwald reports that medical records disclose that Romola had an abortion in 1918, and there are many question marks surrounding this period.

Nijinsky was unhappy with the psychoanalysis and recorded his objections to the doctor's lack of logic in his journal.

Eventually, the seriousness of the situation became clear to Romola. She realised that no progress had been made and that Nijinsky was declining further. There was now no question of him only acting the role of madman. He was tortured by the confusion in his head and needed specialised help. She asked her parents to come to Switzerland to advise her. The doctor was becoming increasingly worried by the responsibility and arranged a consultation with Professor Eugen Bleuler, a famous Zurich psychiatrist, who had introduced his new theory of "schizophrenia" in 1911. Nijinsky was excited at the prospect of discussing his problems, although he wrote, "I am afraid that I will be taken to a lunatic asylum and that I will lose all my work. I have hidden my notebooks." He travelled to Zurich with Romola, optimistically talking about the son they both still wanted.

Romola had the first appointment with Bleuler on her own. She was immensely relieved by his statement at the end:

> *We do not become insane, we are born with it. Genius, insanity, they are so near: normality and abnormality, there is almost no border between the two states .... If you spoke of any other man I might be worried, but the symptoms you describe in the case of an artist and a Russian do not in themselves prove any mental disturbances.*

His buoyant words made his report after he had seen Nijinsky the next day more of a shock. According to Romola's account, Bleuler then told her that her husband was incurably insane and that she should send her child away and get a divorce. When she raced out to where Nijinsky was waiting, he saw it written on her face and said, "*Femmka*, you are bringing me my death warrant."

Ostwald puts it in a different light. He reports that the professor's diagnosis was schizophrenia – confused, with mild manic excitement. Bleuler did not believe that Nijinsky's illness was incurable or that he should be committed to hospitalisation, which could be damaging to Nijinsky's creative sensitivities. He was also against the idea of them having another child because of the risk of inherited mental disease. He recommended that Nijinsky should be encouraged to go his own way and get on with his career – in whatever way he desired as long as it did not harm others.

Nijinsky felt the sword of Damocles descending as he wrote:

> *Death came unexpectedly .... I have been told I am mad. I thought I was alive. They would not let me alone. I lived and rejoiced, but people said I was bad. ... I feel very sad.*
>
> *I know what death is. Death is life extinguished. People who have lost their reason are an extinguished life. I too lacked reason, but when I stayed in St Moritz, I understood, in my room, the whole truth, because I felt a lot. ... only when man is alone can he understand what feeling is.*

It is still a point of contention to his family all these years later that Nijinsky's fate was decided in a mere ten minutes by a practitioner who had just coined the term "schizophrenia". Bleuler's advice to Romola was that she should send Nijinsky to a sanatorium to recover. He suggested Bellevue Kuranstalt in Kreuzlingen (Switzerland), one of the world's leading psychiatric hospitals, directed by Doctor Ludwig Binswanger.

Binswanger was passionately interested in psychoanalysis; he had been trained by Bleuler and Jung and was a lifelong friend of Freud. In that way, he explained, Romola could get on with her own life and Nijinsky could comfortably recover. She did not want to do so and argued with her parents. It was as if Nijinsky deduced the dilemma and responded. They quarrelled; that night, he tried to break into her room in the hotel and then shut himself in his own for twenty-four hours and refused to come out. Romola's parents called the police, and he was taken to the state asylum. He was observed for forty-eight hours and his journals examined. Bleuler felt it unwise for him to return to the hotel, so Nijinsky was escorted to the Bellevue sanatorium.

SUPPRESSION

It was explained to Nijinsky, and he accepted, that it would be beneficial to Romola for them to be separated for a while – that she was nervously exhausted and should rest.

As part of the therapy at Bellevue, it was suggested that he might give another performance. So, on 1 April 1919, Nijinsky "entertained" his last audience of patients, staff and friends. At first, he pounded the piano, and then he performed what Binswanger described as a suicidal madness scene before collapsing, exhausted.

No-one knew what Nijinsky was really thinking. After working through several states of behaviour at the clinic, he expressed a desire to choreograph again. He had ideas for two ballets to the music of Richard Strauss – *Elecktra* and *Symphonia Domestica.* Sadly, neither bore fruit; Nijinsky was in too confused a state and did not have access to the orchestral scores and working materials he needed.

One wonders if providing those creative materials and support would have made a difference, for Nijinsky was cut off from the creative environment in which he had been nurtured for the longest period of his life, without the support of a responsible partner – an Eleonora, a Diaghilev or a Romola. His professional life had finished a day before he was thirty. His aim of retiring from the stage in his early thirties to focus on his choreography and develop a new training for dancers was thwarted by the breakdown of his psyche. He had slipped away into that inner world he had located years before – away from his classmates, Diaghilev,

Romola and the demands of the outer world. The hero had died in the eyes of his public, having survived the highs and lows of notoriety: dismissal from the Imperial Theatre, the adoration of a fawning public, unacceptance of his new ideas for ballet, dismissal from Diaghilev's company for his marriage without notice, ostracisation by the homosexual clique and the crushing failure of his London season. Nijinsky was barred from his home country, dislocated and confused. His spirit stifled and his creativity blocked, he now alternated between acting and psychosis.

DEPENDENCE

Nijinsky's dependence had shifted from Diaghilev to his marriage to Romola, who had been forced to change her role from guru worshipper to manager/agent and, now, to decisionmaker and breadwinner. Whether or not the marriage was a success, he was now solely dependent on her for his survival.

Nijinsky had written in his diary: "I love my wife and Kyra more than anyone." Romola, too, loved her husband, despite the dramatic turn of circumstances. She was still committed to him but was struggling with her own problems, possibly connected to her relationship with the local doctor. Six months after she left Nijinsky at the clinic, she returned to take him home, explaining her turnaround to Binswanger: "I never want to leave him again. I want to nurse him and make his life as agreeable as possible. If I fail to do anything now which might help him, I would never be able to forgive myself later on." She wanted to be back in control of Nijinsky and feared that he would deteriorate by being surrounded by sick people. She also wanted to try the therapy of giving him a son.

Ostwald reports that Binswanger recorded Romola as being herself "severely psychopathic". She was determined to have Nijinsky discharged despite his advice to the contrary. To do so, she was directed to prepare a special room at the Villa Guardament and employ two attendants to care for him.

All was well until Romola became pregnant again and too unwell to supervise him. Nijinsky became out of control and a new attendant reported his condition to the police. He was returned to the Bellevue. Medical records indicate that Nijinsky was very dangerous at the time, violent and acting like an animal. In desperation, Romola sought help from Bleuler, and later from Carl Jung. She wrote that Sigmund Freud told her that his methods were useless for schizophrenia (although Ostwald disputes it). When no-one could give her any useful advice, she took matters into her own hands and moved Nijinsky to the Steinhof Asylum in Vienna, near the clinic where she had given birth to Kyra and wanted to have the new baby.

Their second daughter was born there on 14 June 1920, named Tamara after her father's much-respected professional partner, Tamara Karsavina. She was christened Zsenia Anatazia Marie de la Consolation Madeline.

"There have been many questions about my paternity," Tamara tells me in Phoenix, Arizona, "but I know I am my father's daughter."

The subject is one of the first pieces of unsolicited information offered by her nephew Vaslav Markevitch in our meeting in Italy long after Nijinsky's death: "It was known in Paris," he tells me definitively, "that Tamara was not Nijinsky's daughter. She was the result of my grandmother's affair with Dr Frenkel."

I am embarrassed and uncomfortable. He continues to malign the kind, gentle woman who played host to me in Phoenix, talking continuously and driving. The hot car and discussion are making me sick.

"The baby is not mentioned in Romola's book and in only one line in Bronislava's. The only people to whom it mattered were my mother and grandmother.

Vaslav says that Tamara and Kinga failed to keep an appointment with him in Phoenix and tells me that, at 12.30 am that night, he rang and abused John Gaspers.

His own father had disinherited him – even from his villa, because of a dispute.

We were getting on famously on a marathon exploration of the Tuscan Hills up and down, through fairytale villages, stopping for lunch.

I lie on my bed on this hot Sunday afternoon searching for an understanding of how to tell Nijinsky's story. No, I am not qualified as a member of the family would be, but the quarrelling factions appear to be masking the facts. Why has Tamara not confirmed her paternity with DNA tests and such? And why has Vaslav not contested his rights?

Vaslav says that, undoubtedly, he is the only member of the family to have inherited Nijinsky's gifts, although he concedes his son Leo has to some degree.

> *Nijinsky was not easy to understand because of being a heavenly creature – like Jupiter coming down to earth to lead a normal life. He knew things and it was hard to understand because he did not share a language with many people – a little French, less English, little German and he was surrounded by Russians most of his life.*

He then became accusative: "But you have no culture, you Australians. You mix the deeply important with the superficial. You should realise that you will have to suffer to write about Nijinsky. Nijinsky knew that one has to suffer in order to achieve."

Vaslav is becoming more aggressive. I feel cornered and take some time out to breathe in the garden with his cat.

I am too nervous about his mood swings to insist that this is what I'm trying to do – to make Nijinsky and his world accessible. He stamps off, saying, no-one has offered to help him get his own book out.

He finally drives me home.

I am reeling from the persecution, and I explore means of taking a train out that night. Alas, I fail to find any means of transport. I eat at the hotel with the farmers – the only non-Italian in the room.

The next morning brings him back unabashed.

He says, "We can still do something good together for Nijinsky," and begins arranging for me to look over the Berenson house outside Florence, where he was brought up – now a stately home. Then, he says, I will understand him. (Is this the house that should have been his?)

He doesn't apologise but says I have copped the end of people pilfering his information, and he is happy to help me after his book is published but not before. He has been prevented by the occult. He says he is willing to help me and Paul Cox with the best-ever film. Another one? Paul's film was launched in 2001.

After Nijinsky's breakdown, Romola's life was heavy with responsibility. She was an extraordinarily determined woman who was now obsessed with finding a cure for her husband and constantly on the search for answers in the fast-developing new field of psychiatry. She tried everything, resorting to both religious and alternative methods, including Christian Science; she took Nijinsky to faith healers and on a pilgrimage to Lourdes.

In desperation, she smuggled a letter to Bronislava into Russia. The new Union of Soviet States of Russia had been established and Lenin was the new prime minister. Bronislava was now separated from her husband, living in Kyiv with her mother and children, successfully running a school, Ecole de Mouvement, teaching Nijinsky's methods. Nijinsky had been earlier assured that they were safe and well and had sent them money. They also learnt that Stassik had died from a liver complaint in the sanatorium. When he was told the news, Nijinsky smiled in a strange, melancholic way, as he had when his father had died, at the same time consoling Romola: "Do not cry; he was insane; it is better like this."

Bronislava was shocked when she read that her brother was seriously mentally ill. She was unable to leave the Soviet Union (as it was then known) immediately but took huge risks in illegally escaping with her mother and two children the following year. It took them six weeks travelling to finally reach Vienna in May 1921. It was a happy experience for Bronislava to finally introduce her two children, Irina, seven, and Leo, two, to the family and to meet Nijinsky's children Kyra, seven, and Tamara, one, but she and her mother were devastated when Nijinsky did not recognise them. He, who had been her soul mate all her life, remained withdrawn until Bronislava said something to him about the ballets she had devised for her students. Suddenly, he sparked up. "The ballet is never devised; the ballet must be created." It was enough to convince her that her brother was completely sane, a sign that his problems were only temporary.

The two women in Nijinsky's life (excluding his mother) were totally different in character and argued: Eleonora and Bronislava thought Romola extravagant and wasteful of Nijinsky's money. Bronislava had arrived in Austria penniless and destitute, dependent on Romola for board and lodging. In order to reestablish her career in the West, she contacted Diaghilev with an offer to work with the Ballets Russes. She was greatly relieved when he accepted her offer, but the news was badly received by Romola, who was outraged that her husband's sister would consider joining forces with the person she held partly responsible for his state.

Bronislava immediately left for London to begin her new career. She intended to stage her brother's works and was shocked to discover how fast his name was fading and how little of his ideas the dancers had absorbed, particularly when Diaghilev asked her to revive his *L'Apres-midi d'un faune.* She immediately began to record her memories of Nijinsky's contributions to the history of dance, which were completed by her daughter after her death and published as *Bronislava Nijinska: Early Memoirs* in 1981.

During the next five decades, Bronislava perpetuated the Nijinsky name by exerting her own influence on dance. It was widespread. She reinvigorated the Ballets Russes and fulfilled her early promise by becoming a major choreographer in her own right. Bronislava created over seventy ballets, plus new dances for the revival of *The Sleeping Beauty – Aurora's Wedding* – in 1922 and several major works for the Ballets Russes: *Les noces*, which had been originally intended for Nijinsky to work on with Stravinsky, *Le train bleu* and *Les biches*, which was developed from Nijinsky's earlier work in *Jeux*. Bronislava (known as Nijinska) also introduced a new talent from Russia to the Ballets Russes – Serge Lifar, a young dancer whom she had trained in Kyiv.

In 1924, Diaghilev recognised George Balanchine's potential as a choreographer and, in typical fashion, spontaneously invited him and the three other members of his company to join the Ballets Russes. His move upset Bronislava, who did not believe that there was room for them both. She immediately left the company and began to forge a freelance career, choreographing new works for the Paris Opera and Teatro Colon in Buenos Aires. In 1928, she became artistic director and choreographer of the Ida Rubenstein Ballet (the company founded by the unknown dancer brought to fame by Diaghilev in *Cléopâtre*) before forming her own company, Ballets Nijinska, in 1932 and in 1937, Bronislava became artistic director and choreographer of the Polish Ballet. She went on to establish her own school in Hollywood in 1939 and worked with the American Ballet Theatre for its inaugural season that year. Among her long list of achievements across the world, one of the highlights was demonstrating Nijinsky's *L'Apres-midi d'un faune* to the Kirov Ballet in London in 1970.

DESPERATION

Romola had been teetering financially for the last few years and was running out of money again. She had many demands and few resources. Her sister Tessa's marriage had failed, and she had become dependent on her. Romola had her two children and their household staff to support on top of Nijinsky's care in the institution. She managed to secure the last of Nijinsky's money from Russia and tried to obtain work as an actress. She renewed acquaintance with the director of the Paris Opera, who had offered Nijinsky a job when he left the Ballets Russes, in an effort to act as Bronislava's agent. Romola did succeed in obtaining an advance for Bronislava on her contract to produce Nijinsky's works and choreograph new ballets. Romola also instigated the first of many lawsuits over her husband's rights. She lodged a claim against Diaghilev for unpaid debts from Nijinsky's last performances in America.

A chance remark of Nijinsky's about how much he loved America set Romola on a campaign to live and work in the United States, but the country would not accept mentally ill immigrants. She was determined to find a solution and, in the meantime, rented a flat in Paris and continued to search for a means of generating an income. Although she was inexperienced at earning a living, Romola was tenacious and enterprising. She borrowed capital from her family and attempted nine different commercial ventures, including a taxi business and a pastry shop. All of them failed. She was continually forced to ask her long-suffering parents for more money.

Diaghilev may have also prayed for a miracle. Irrespective of the crippling blow he had delivered his former lover at the time of his marriage, Diaghilev felt compassion for him and may have harboured regret for his harsh reaction – although he had dealt the same treatment to Massine. It is highly unlikely that either his action or the marriage to Romola caused Nijinsky's mental decline, but for whatever reason, Diaghilev kept in sporadic touch with Romola and tried to help Nijinsky return to reality. In 1922, he invited him to a rehearsal and had the orchestra play the music of *Le Sacre du printemps.* At the time, the Ballets Russes was enjoying a revival – helped out by Bronislava and the reproduction of *The Sleeping Princess* and *Aurora's Wedding* for Petipa's centenary year. At first Nijinsky, responded to the music, but he soon relapsed into his remote world.

Lifar was a loyal support to the Nijinsky family. He had never worked with Nijinsky but owed his lifestyle and career in the West to Bronislava, who had been his former teacher in the Soviet Union. Lifar wrote in his biography that Diaghilev refused to reconcile himself with Nijinsky's misfortune and never abandoned hope that some shock would restore him to the world. He tells of how Diaghilev had visited Nijinsky at the Paris flat early in his illness and asked him to return to work with the company, to which Nijinsky allegedly calmly replied, "I cannot because I am mad."

Two years later, in 1924, Diaghilev again attempted to help Nijinsky by inviting him to rehearsals of his sister's ballet *Le train bleu,* conceived by Cocteau and designed by Coco Chanel as a showcase for the acrobatic skills of the company's new star, Anton Dolin. To Bronislava's devastation, Nijinsky sat expressionless through the entire ballet. Knowing how he would have previously been fascinated by the choreography, Bronislava broke down, finally realising that her brother was unlikely to return to his former self.

Dolin, too, insisted on meeting his idol and, as a celebratory present for the opening of *Le train bleu,* rather than the Cartier jewellery suggested by Diaghilev, he forced him into arranging a visit to the Nijinsky flat. It took three days of Dolin refusing to speak to

Diaghilev for him to give in to his protégé's consuming desire to meet the man on whom he had built all his ideals and whose roles he was performing in the Ballets Russes and in Diaghilev's personal life. Dolin writes of visiting Nijinsky, Romola and his two daughters in their small suburban apartment at Neuilly, on the outskirts of Paris. He was very shaken by the experience – disconcerted that Nijinsky's brain refused to work, despite the fact that he looked in perfect health.

Nijinsky understood, Dolin wrote, but was unable to communicate.

> *I have often wondered what Diaghilev's feelings were at that meeting, but whatever they were, he succeeded in hiding them. During tea Nijinsky neither ate nor drank and seemed powerless to do anything. He sat in his chair as though he was trying to understand. I believe he did comprehend a great deal, but there was no communication …. At last we rose to go, Diaghilev embraced Nijinsky. By this time, I was feeling the strain and could hardly hold out my hand to say goodbye. I put my arms on my shoulders. Perhaps it was my fancy, but he seemed to resent it. After a moment, however, he put a hand on my shoulder and kissed me three times, as all Russians do on parting. He came to the door with us and said goodbye in Russian and when Diaghilev asked if we might come again, he simply shook his head wistfully, as if to say, "I am very tired."*

Romola moved the family to a larger apartment in Avenue de la Bourdonnais, but eventually ran out of resources in 1925 and made the decision to disband the family. Kyra was having ballet lessons at the Paris Opera and taking part in a few ballets, but Romola was worried that she might be displaying the same symptoms as her father. She was advised by Bleuler that it was not a case of mental illness but an abnormality of character and that, if the same symptoms persisted, Kyra should be raised outside the family.

Romola arranged for Kyra to be sent to an exclusive boarding school in Switzerland, paid for by her grandparents, and sent Tamara to live with them in Budapest. However, Kyra was not happy in the mountains and went to join her sister. The reunion did not last for long: Romola was begged to let Kyra be brought up in New York by a childless rich hotelier and his wife, who initially nurtured her and encouraged her ballet but later abandoned her.

In 1926, the segregation of the Nijinsky family took on a more permanent status when Romola moved to the United States, leaving Nijinsky in the care of her sister Tessa.

LEAVING PHOENIX

Kinga has taken it upon herself to put the record straight on her controversial, iron-willed grandmother. She strongly relates to her and both she and her mother have inherited some of that iron will.

I farewell the Nijinskys amicably, laden with Nijinsky memorabilia – a pendant and brooch. I feel accepted into the side. I come away with increased awareness of the interest in Nijinsky but not many more insights into his soul. I have gained much ancillary information, such as the sad demise of the eldest daughter Kyra – the former apple of her father's eye, the promising dancer who conversely married Diaghilev's last protégé, Igor Markevitch, worked with him in the Italian Resistance during the Second World War, divorced and immigrated to San Francisco, lived in poverty there in her declining years, estranged from her family and finally joining the Franciscan movement and wearing the robe in which she was buried. Tamara sadly explains that the sisters only reunited at her death. I discover that Kyra has a son living in Europe. When I show interest in contacting him and his children, I am told again not to do so. "He's mad; they are all mad," I'm told. But he Is part of the Nijinsky story and cannot be ignored.

I have learnt much about Romola – how she travelled, leaving her children behind, with Kyra passed around and for a time in boarding school and Tamara in the care of her mother and stepfather.

DEMISE

In 1928, Diaghilev made a further attempt to help Nijinsky. Ironically, whether intentionally or not, Diaghilev introduced all of Nijinsky's replacements to him. This time, he took Lifar to visit Nijinsky at his Passy apartment in Paris, where Tessa was caring for him.

Lifar reports that Nijinsky was lying on a low mattress wearing a dressing gown, "either biting his nails till the blood came or somewhat affectedly playing with his wrists". When he approached and kissed Nijinsky's hand, "for a moment, his eyes glowered at me from under the knitted brows with the wild, suspicious glance of a hunted animal, then quite suddenly, a wonderful smile lit up his face, a smile so kindly, so childishly pure, so luminous and undimmed, that I feel utterly under its charm". Diaghilev boasted about Lifar's jump in his role of the Moor in *Petrushka*, which he planned to take Nijinsky to that night. He measured them against each other and found Nijinsky to be half a head shorter. Lifar wrote in his book that he believed the reason for Nijinsky's demise to be because he had been set on too high a pinnacle.

That evening, Diaghilev took Nijinsky to a performance of *Petrushka* at the Paris Opera in the hope that the experience of seeing the ballet performed by his former partner Karsavina might shock him out of his mental disorder. They sat together in a box and went on stage during the second interval to be photographed with Diaghilev, Karsavina, Lifar, Benois and other members of the company. Karsavina was very upset. She described her reaction:

> *I saw vacant eyes and a passive shuffling gait, and stepped forward to kiss Nijinsky. A shy smile lit up his face and his eyes looked straight into mine. I thought he knew me, and I was afraid to speak lest it interrupt a slow-forming thought. He kept silent. I then called him by his pet name, "Vatza!" He dropped his head and slowly turned it away. Nijinsky meekly let himself be led to where the photographers had set their cameras. I put my arm through his, and, requested to look straight into the camera, I could not see his movements. I noticed the photographers were hesitating, and, looking round, saw that Nijinsky was leaning forward and looking into my face, but on meeting my eyes he again turned his head like a child that wants to hide tears. And that pathetic, shy, helpless movement went straight to my heart.*

It was the same night that Diaghilev was introduced to his last protégé – the slim, handsome Igor Markevitch from Kyiv, who was only sixteen at the time. Diaghilev was impressed by Markevitch's talent and intellect. He encouraged him to compose a concerto and to perform it at the Royal Opera House, Covent Garden. It was too early in Markevitch's career and not a great success, but Diaghilev nevertheless commissioned him to compose the music for a ballet based on Hans Andersen's story "The Emperor's New Clothes", called *Les habits neufs du roi*. Markevitch intended to integrate speech and aleatory music (improvised music) into the work, which would have been virtually impossible for dancers, but it was never written.

Diaghilev's health was fast deteriorating. He was suffering from diabetes and had been instructed to rest, but it was not in his character. His energy was flagging and he was becoming foul-mouthed and decadent. He became given to uncontrollable rages. Diaghilev's close friend Misia Sert observed that "his aloofness was becoming more pronounced and he was vainer than ever, munching chocolates and sniffing cocaine". Grigoriev had noticed for some time that Diaghilev was losing enthusiasm for ballet. He was despondent at not finding a collaborator to succeed him at the Ballets Russes who met his ideals. He had decided against Lifar and was leaning on his secretary/companion Kochno for artistic advice and intellectual comfort. Diaghilev eventually acknowledged Kochno as his chosen successor, referring to him as the "Young Oak".

Diaghilev's major passion had shifted to rare book collecting and, as with everything he embarked on in his life, he spared no effort or expense. He was overjoyed to be left a letter written by Pushkin in the will of a descendant and persuaded the grand duke who inherited the remaining ten to sell them to him too.

On the evening of a gala in honour of King Fuad of Egypt on 24 July 1929, Diaghilev saw his company dance for the last time. Backstage after the show, he farewelled them and thanked them for their year's work, telling them he would see them after the holiday break. It was obvious to the dancers that he was unwell, and tears were streaming down some of their faces. Diaghilev left for Paris the next day, and the Ballets Russes gave its final performance for the year on 4 August at Vichy. No-one was aware at the time that it was the company's last-ever performance.

Rather than the rest cure his doctor had recommended, Diaghilev then embarked on a strenuous cultural pilgrimage to Munich, the Salzburg Festival and Baden-Baden with Markevitch, glorying in his great love of music. During an interval of *Tristan and Isolde* at the Prinzregententheater in Munich, he went out into the garden with Markevitch and started to cry: "I said it to you in London – everything is too beautiful."

Diaghilev travelled on to join Lifar at his usual holiday place at the Grand Hotel de Bains on the Lido in Venice, which he seemed to have discounted as being on the water as the gypsy had prophesied years before. His health was in a bad state and he immediately took to his bed. Lifar nursed him day and night. At Diaghilev's urging, Lifar sent three telegrams to Kochno within twenty- four hours. The first read *The weather is beautiful. Do not forget me*. The next morning: *Health not very good. When do you plan on coming?* And that evening: *Am sick. Come at once*. He also had Misia Sert called to his bedside by telegram. When she arrived with Coco Chanel, Misia was distressed to find Diaghilev shivering in bed in his dinner jacket despite the sweltering heat. They were more shocked when he sang Tchaikovsky's *Pathetique* at the top of his voice and uncharacteristically confided to them that it and *Triston and Isolde* had been his lifelong favourites.

Diaghilev died on 19 August surrounded by Boris Kochno, Serge Lifar, Misia Sert and Coco Chanel.

At the moment of the maestro's last breath, a bizarre scene took place: Kochno and Lifar fell on Diaghilev's body, fighting each other as jealously as they had vied for his attention during his life. Misia described them as like mad dogs fighting over the body of their master, and at his funeral, they both crawled on their knees towards the open grave where Diaghilev's coffin had been lowered in the Russian cemetery on Isola di San Michele.

Lifar and Balanchine made the last years of the Ballets Russes memorable. Lifar was close enough to Diaghilev to be admitted to his charmed circle, and the collaboration between Balanchine – Diaghilev's last and greatest choreographer – and his great musical discovery Stravinsky is charted as one of the most glorious in ballet history and one of the most important parts of the vast Diaghilev legacy.

By combining great painting, music and choreography, Diaghilev developed an art form with more range of expression than ever in history. Ballets Russes was a synthesis of all the arts. His friends were people – mostly men, apart from Misia Sert – of exceptional talent whom he either guided and developed or exchanged ideas with. He was a collector and nurturer of artists (and later books), composers, painters, dancers and choreographers. His vision for combining the arts in lavish spectacles has benefited them individually and collectively and opened them up to a wider audience. Diaghilev bequeathed a wealth of uncompromising ideas and ideals that have informed and nourished the arts up to the present day. His ideas are a monument to his personal aesthetic taste. What a man! Diaghilev changed many lives – a lover of beauty who intuitively recognised talent and devoted his life to fostering it and displaying it to the world. He expected little in return apart from his right to shape the final product. Despite his pioneering of the creative team, he was always the string-puller, the mastermind, the executive director. After Fokine left the Ballets Russes, Diaghilev took on the joint roles of choreographer and director of the company, commissioning artists to implement his ideas. In his constant search for the new, Diaghilev became more interested in the works of the French avant-garde during the 1920s. He remained as he described himself as a young man in 1897 until the time of his death:

> *I am first a charlatan, but a brilliant one; secondly a great charmer; thirdly a man with a great deal of logic, but very few principles. Lastly, I am a lout. I think I have found my true vocation – a Maecanas. I have all that is necessary except the money, mais ça viendra.*

DISPARATE LIVES

Diaghilev's first star was oblivious to his demise, incarcerated in his small apartment in Paris, neglected by Romola and her sister Tessa, whose care he was supposedly under. In 1929, Romola arranged for Nijinsky to be readmitted to the Bellevue, which she had attempted a couple of other times but Tessa had cancelled because of his 'excited' state.

The members of Nijinsky's dispersed family were leading disparate lives. Kyra was the only one to follow in her father's family footsteps in becoming a dancer. She had shown early promise and, at the instigation of Romola, was sponsored by friends to study in several major cities. She was multilingual and spoke Italian, German, French and some Hungarian. Kyra considered herself her father's reincarnation – the upholder of his legacy. She choreographed and danced in a ballet to his original idea of Liszt's *Mephisto-Walzer* and spoke on the radio of how her father had confided in her the secrets of the art of dance, of how "to dance, to dance, to embrace the entire world … that is my plan". Like him, she lived within herself, although unlike him, she was vivacious and articulate. She liked to dance alone (which was the name of a film made about her in the 1980s). Kyra never really rejoined the family until her last few years – after their disbanding in 1925, she was cut off from them until her marriage in 1936. By a strange quirk of fate, Kyra's bridegroom was Diaghilev's last protégé, Igor Markevitch, who had become the famous conductor predicted by

Diaghilev. And as if a further endorsement of synchronicity – the circle of life her father advocated – Kyra's witness at the wedding on 24 April was her father's former partner, Tamara Karsavina, whose husband was the British ambassador to Hungary.

In January of the following year, Kyra gave birth to a son, Vaslav. She suffered huge deprivation in Italy during the war years, being captured by Nazis and accused of being a spy. After the Allies took over Europe, she was appointed director and dancer at the Opera in Florence but lost custody of her son to Igor in 1948. She moved to California in the late 1950s, where she painted and wrote poetry.

Ironically, Markevitch was appointed executor of Nijinsky's estate, presumably by Romola. In John Drummond's fascinating book *Speaking of Diaghilev,* he recounts an incident Markevitch told him of his son Vaslav when, as a teenager, he was playing on the beach of The Lido in Venice and an elderly observer remarked how much he resembled a Russian dancer who used to visit there in the early 1900s.

Tamara was almost a hidden secret – unmentioned in either of her mother's books and granted only one line in Richard Buckle's biography of her father. Despite her verbal loyalty to her mother when talking of her, she never bonded with her and was brought up by her grandparents in Budapest.

Tamara grew up hardly knowing her mother or father, although she said her grandmother always talked about him with respect as an artist, even though she had not been happy with Romola marrying him and fainted at the news: "She had a premonition that something would go terribly wrong."

Tamara's first memories of her father were of sitting on the knee of a kindly man who offered her the treat of *un canard* – a sugar lump dipped in coffee. She writes of the rare occasions when he was in the drawing room: "I would climb up on his lap and thrill over the protective way he would place his left arm around me. It was as though an unspoken conspiracy developed between us. We did not need words to communicate with each other." There were later visits to his nursing home in Switzerland, but Tamara said:

> *It was not the great Nijinsky – it was a human being who was not in this world. Each time I saw him he was smiling. He must have realized deep down that I was his daughter. They tell me that when I was born in Vienna, he was in and out of the sanatorium. They couldn't find me and then they saw me in Father's arms walking up and down.*

Tamara was later told Romola had cast her aside because she didn't want her to suffer the stigma of a mentally ill father. There was controversy over her birth because of her father's state at the time of her conception and her mother's comforting relationship with the local doctor. It could only have been resolved by genetic tests.

Tamara was officially adopted by her grandmother in her teens to make her eligible for a scholarship to the national drama school in Hungary. It provoked a furious reaction from Romola. She forbade Tamara to use the name Nijinsky and later followed it up with legal action. Whatever the distortions of the truth, photographs reveal a pronounced physical resemblance between Bronislava and Tamara.

In August 1944, Tamara married Miklos Szakats, a fellow actor, whom she had met at the National Drama School in Budapest. Szakats was an actor of smouldering charisma whose photo still produces swoon reactions today. It was not a long-lasting union but gave birth to a daughter Kinga – named after the visionary medieval Hungarian Princess Kinga (who married a Polish prince and is credited with mystically transferring a rich resource of salt mines into the country) – the second of Nijinsky's two grandchildren.

Romola travelled constantly, spending the majority of her time in the United States. She was a volatile and reactionary character who lavished love when she found it and explored many ways of life – she embraced spiritualism and lesbian relationships. She was always tender to her husband and devoted to his cause, but only saw him every few years and had little to do with her family. Romola fought a constant battle to keep Nijinsky's name alive to raise funds for his hospitalisation. She was not always able to pay her bills but was a brilliant organiser. Her major goal was to organise a foundation to support him in the sanatorium and secure his future. It was for that reason that she embarked on writing his biography with the help of several collaborators – particularly Lincoln Kirstein, who was involved with founding the Ballet Theater, now the American Ballet Theater. She dedicated the book to her lover Frederica Dezentje, who died just before the book was published in 1933. The book created a crisis with her mother, who felt maligned, but not everybody shared her thoughts; Una – Lady Troubridge – wrote to Romola saying the book was a great tribute and vowed to "never to see another ballet, until I can see Nijinsky dance in heaven".

INSIGHTS

Romola arranged for Nijinsky's drawings to be exhibited, and when she found his forgotten notebooks in a trunk, she saw them as a further opportunity to both raise money and maintain his name. But the result of her action reached far further: the publishing of Nijinsky's notebooks revealed the first true insights into his psyche. Romola launched into translating and editing the candid documents, inviting eminent psychiatrist Alfred Adler to write the preface. Adler accepted, but Romola chose not to publish his view that Nijinsky's illness "sprang from a deep inferiority complex; that he developed grandiose expectations during his childhood ... was constantly disappointed because life was not like childhood dreams".

Romola then asked Carl Jung, but he was not prepared to comment without meeting Nijinsky, so Romola wrote her own introduction for *The Diary of Vaslav Nijinsky,* which was published in 1936.

Romola had edited the four notebooks into a single narrative, and the book was an immediate success, despite the fact that Nijinsky's ideas on love, religion and life were distorted by her heavy editing. It was not known at the time that she had cut out large chunks – over thirty thousand words – mostly on sex and bodily functions.

Although it was a sanitised version of Nijinsky's thoughts and left out a large amount of his words, the book had an impact beyond the usual autobiography of a legendary star. It was a crucial document in changing widely held perceptions of Nijinsky and for its rare insights into a creative mind on the brink of insanity. The fact that his thoughts on his performing life were written retrospectively in a short period makes it both a moving self-analysis and a valuable case study. It explained much about Nijinsky's life and revealed his complex, intuitive and intelligent personality rather than the single-dimensional, introverted, inarticulate man often written off as an idiot.

More of the inner workings of Nijinsky's mind were revealed when the unexpurgated edition was finally published through the efforts of his daughter Tamara in French in 1995 and English in 1999 and through subsequent vehicles such as Australian filmmaker Paul Cox's film in 2001.

Nijinsky's rambling style revealed a rich inner poetry. Nijinsky's thoughts on the page link to his expression on stage – the riveting performer, the *expresser extraordinaire* of grace, poetry and dynamic energy. Together with the deeply etched interpretations of his dancing roles and his radical choreography, the diary disclosed Nijinsky's depth of thinking and strength of intelligence and perception. It revealed the workings of his quick, restless and highly cultured mind, reacting with intensity to the events and people around him. His former son-in-law and executor of his estate, Igor Markevitch, has compared Nijinsky's writing to the stream-of-consciousness narration of James Joyce's *Ulysses.*

His major subjects included Diaghilev, Romola, religion, politics and his Tolstoyan philosophies. He dwelt on the sayings of Nietzsche, Darwin, Maupassant and other thinkers and philosophers. It puts paid to misconceptions such as Nijinsky's lack of understanding of music. Nijinsky was dismissed as a musical ignoramus by people such as Stravinsky, yet Bronislava Nijinsky wrote about her brother's early compositions and his ability to play whole sonatas from memory. He performed complete pieces perfectly without anyone realising that he could not read music.

He writes: "Intellectual music is a machine. Music with feeling is God." It makes Nijinsky's groundbreaking choreography, which worked the dance through the beat of the music, even more of an achievement. He was either working completely out of his head or instinct – or both – as no-one had previously introduced such concepts. Yet, as Lynn Garafola points out in her erudite analytic book *Diaghilev's Ballets Russes*, the diary disappointingly reveals no clues to the origin of his choreography.

SHOCKS

As Romola roamed the world, Nijinsky was in and out of sanatoriums. In 1937, he was visited by his children, whom he had not seen for ten years, although his son-in-law Markevitch had tried and been turned away by the authorities at the clinic, who were under instructions to only allow visitors with written permission from Nijinsky's wife.

Nijinsky's general condition was deteriorating; his physical health was failing, exacerbating his unstable mental health. He had developed high blood pressure and suffered two heart attacks within a year. Across the world in America, Romola was relentless in pursuing her crusade for a cure. She had come across a radical insulin shock treatment claimed to cure schizophrenia. The Bellevue administrators were reluctant to take the risk, particularly after Nijinsky's heart attacks. The treatment was in its early stages of development and very expensive, but Romola was very keen to try it on her husband. She turned to her Nijinsky friends and supporters in London for help.

As a result, Tamara Karsavina, Anton Dolin and Lady Diana Cooper, with Lady Juliet Duff as chairman, formed the Nijinsky Foundation in London in 1937. A special Nijinsky matinee was arranged at His Majesty's Theatre on 28 May 1936 to launch the project. Taking part were Margot Fonteyn, Robert Helpmann, Alicia Markova, Frederick Ashton, Mary Honer and Harold

Turner, Serge Lifar and John Gielgud, who recited a poem specially written for the occasion.

Two years later, against Bellevue head Binswanger's advice, Romola moved Nijinsky to another clinic to begin his first course of insulin treatments. After forty- eight treatments, there was no marked medical improvement, but Romola was convinced that there was and reported so to the press. Lifar organised a fund-raising gala for the Nijinsky Foundation in Paris, and Romola arranged for him to visit Nijinsky in the clinic with a group of press photographers in June 1939. Lifar reported Nijinsky to be markedly improved, despite his distorted speech and erratic physical behaviour. Although still confused, Nijinsky obliged requests to perform his famous leap as a public demonstration of his recovery, much to the chagrin of the clinic authorities. Lifar joined him in the session of jumping and a little dancing orchestrated for the photographers. The hospital reported Nijinsky slightly improved after the visit, but the controversial protocol was eventually stopped after two hundred and twenty-eight treatments.

ACT 2

With the prospect of another world war, Romola stepped up efforts to live permanently in the United States. She had been spending tracts of time there since 1926 and was eventually granted permission, but the American Consul in Berne refused to recognise Nijinsky's Swiss "Nansen" (stateless person's) passport and blocked his entry.

So the Nijinskys were once again stranded in Europe at the declaration of the Second World War. Nijinsky had a moment of heartwarming clarity at its onset when he turned to Romola and said, "Act 2 begins," but the Nijinskys were facing the insecure life of refugees, handicapped by the fact that Nijinsky was now an invalid living within himself and totally dependent on Romola's wits. Although Romola chose to report Nijinsky's alleged statements to the press, other people reported him to be incapable of conversation. Nijinsky had retreated from the external world and only spoke occasionally. Because they could not both immigrate to the United States, Romola was forced to settle her differences with her mother over the references to her in *The Diary of Vaslav Nijinsky* and again accept her hospitality. They moved into the top floor of Emilia Markus and Oscar Pardany's house in Budapest in July 1940, but there was soon another falling out and Nijinsky was moved to the state asylum.

In Budapest, Romola resumed contact with a wealthy, socially connected second cousin, Paul Bohus Vilagosi, whom she had met some years before. Ostwald writes that Paul said he was in love with Romola and seems to have been equally in love with Nijinsky. Vilagosi proved a loyal companion and valuable support to Romola for the rest of her life.

During the 1944 German occupation of Budapest, Vilagosi arranged for the three of them to take refuge in the small town of Sopron, on the shores of Lake Neuiedler near the Austrian border. Luckily, they found a place for Nijinsky in the local hospital. However, it developed into a problem when the Nazis stepped up their campaign to annihilate "inferior" people such as Jews, Romani and the insane. Romola and Vilagosi were surprised by Nijinsky's arrival on the doorstep one morning, delivered by his trusted hospital attendant. By a stroke of luck, the attendant had heard that the Germans had accelerated efforts to track down the mentally ill and scheduled liquidation of the insane for the following morning. Romola writes: "There stood Vaslav in his old gray woollen coat, wearing his little Tyrolean hat and carrying a bundle in which his clothes and belongings were wrapped."

The Russian army was fast approaching the town. The Nijinsky group had no choice but to flee the invasion but was apprehended and accused of being Russian spies. Somehow, they managed to extricate themselves and hide in caves under the Carmelite Convent with several thousand people during the Russian bombing. During this period, Romola reports Nijinsky as calm and compliant, in contrast to the turmoil in the caves. When they returned to the town, the group found it to have been taken over by Russian soldiers, who were occupying the house in which they had been living.

The Russian occupation pierced Nijinsky's clouded consciousness. The sights and sounds of his home countrymen triggered dormant reactions. When he was addressed in French by one of the soldiers, Nijinsky immediately responded in Russian, saying, "Take it easy." The Russian soldiers were overawed when they realised they were in the presence of the legendary Nijinsky. One night, as they were singing and drinking, Nijinsky suddenly responded to the familiar music, flinging himself into their circle and leaping into dance.

At the end of the war, Romola was faced with the dilemma of where they should live. She eventually decided on Vienna, as it was an international zone divided between the Russians, Americans, British and French. As always, she maximised her contacts and resources to secure a luxurious suite of rooms at the famous Sacher Hotel. Romola borrowed a car from the Red Cross to collect Nijinsky, but they suffered another ordeal when they were taken prisoner by the Russians on the way back.

The Nijinskys were eventually rescued by an English balletomane posted to the Allied Commission, Mrs Margaret Power, who had been asked to find them by friends in London. She provided food and arranged for them to access money from the Nijinsky fund. The hotel was then requisitioned by the British Army, but Romola persuaded the army authorities to let them stay and to provide them with a hot meal every day. Despite the temporary nature of the arrangement and their restricted conditions, life in the comparatively luxurious hotel was a great bonus after the trials of life on the run.

The sojourn in Vienna offered them the opportunity to absorb themselves in culture again. Romola and Nijinsky frequented exhibitions and concerts, which Nijinsky appeared to enjoy. As a surprise gift from the Russian Kommandatura in Vienna, the Nijinskys were invited to a performance by the Leningrad Ballet (as the Imperial Ballet was then called in Europe) starring Galina Ulanova and finishing with *Les Sylphides*, Romola noted the obvious enjoyment on her husband's face. The next day, Romola took him to visit Ulanova. Nijinsky had known her in Russia, and her parents had been his former classmates in St Petersburg.

All the time, Romola was desperately chasing visas and searching for a more permanent home for them. When they were finally forced to leave the hotel, in desperation she begged for help from the American Provost Marshall, Colonel Yarborough. He generously provided them with a car and pass to look for temporary accommodation in the American zone. They were lucky to discover an unoccupied fairytale 11th-century castle, Castle Mittersill, high in the mountains of Austria near the Grossglockner, between Kitzbuhel and Zell am See. They took refuge in the idyllic environment while Romola and Vilagosi desperately continued their search.

ENGLAND

Having exhausted avenues to live in Paris or immigrate to America, the Nijinskys finally obtained permission to live in England. They arrived in November 1947 to stay in a house in the country lent by one of their friends and supporters. Through the generosity of the group, they were able to live comfortably in a succession of borrowed abodes.

Romola persisted in taking Nijinsky to cultural events and creating fundraising opportunities around him. A second gala for the Nijinsky Foundation was organised in London in November 1949, with Toumanova, Chauviré, Babilée, Tallchief, Massine and Skouratoff participating. Nijinsky was expected to attend, but at the last minute, the organisers were sent word that he was not in a fit state.

In early 1950, Lifar requested Nijinsky's appearance at a special event at the Paris Opera Ballet, of which he was director. At the beginning of April, Lifar invited the Nijinskys to a rehearsal for a television performance of his company. Nijinsky appeared to enjoy the experience and Romola noticed him making dance movements later as if choreographing. The next day, Romola was alarmed by the deterioration in his health. She called a couple of doctors and then his consultant in Switzerland and finally took him to a clinic. Nijinsky's kidneys had failed. On 8 April 1950, the hero of the Diaghilev stage lapsed into a coma and exited unceremoniously from the wings of the world.

Nijinsky's long vigil was over, but in the eyes of the world, the curtain had come down on him thirty years before. He was fifty-nine years old but had withered offstage since 1919, when he was twenty-nine, apart from the two bizarre performances at Suvetia House and in the asylum. Nijinsky had been declared insane at the peak of his performing career and formative stage as a choreographer. Like his fellow geniuses Mozart and Schubert, he had died young, but unlike them, he had endured a sad thirty-one more mortal years.

Nijinsky's passing was marked by a requiem mass at St James in Spanish Place, London, and he was buried in Marylebone Cemetery. The chosen pallbearers were Michael Soames, Anton Dolin, Serge Lifar, Richard Buckle, George Raymond, Frederick Ashton and George Balanchine (who failed to arrive).

PARIS

Nijinsky had died penniless, and Romola was drained financially. She handed the legal authority over to Lifar to arrange the transfer of him bodily back to Paris, the city of his greatest triumphs. The date was finally set for 4 June 1953. Nijinsky's remains were exhumed and he was dressed in the silk bonnet and arm bracelets of *Le Spectre de la rose*, in which he had thrilled so many audiences across the globe. Yet his most persistent fan did not accompany him on his last trip. Romola was in the midst of the process of finally qualifying for permanent residence in America and was advised by solicitors not to leave the country.

Instead, as if a testimony to the circle of life he advocated, Nijinsky was farewelled from England by Nadia Nicolaevna Legat, the second wife of his mentor, Nicolas Legat, who had endorsed his entry to the Imperial School. Nadia was working in England as the head of a ballet school in Tunbridge Wells. She guarded and decorated the coffin with her pupils, staying with her husband's famous protégé until he left on his final journey to France.

In Paris, Nijinsky's coffin was met by more of the major players of his past: his sister Bronislava, his former partner Mathilde Kschessinska with her husband the Grand Duke Andre and her son, Olga Preobrajenska and many other Russian émigrés. Lifar laid a wreath on the coffin. Together with dancers from the Paris Opera School and Ballet, they lovingly laid him to rest in the cemetery at Montmartre, near Auguste Vestris, his predecessor as God of the Dance.

EPILOGUE

So the Diaghilev era, the most brilliant in ballet history, drew to a close with the death of its major star. In the short span of his illustrious career – a mere ten years – Nijinsky had achieved much: he turned around the status of dance in the Western world, created a new role for the male dancer and pushed the barriers of the art form with his neoclassical choreography. The great God of Dance was out of step with his time – a legend in his own lifetime. Despite the efforts of his wife to keep his name alive, few people in the 21st century are aware that Nijinsky lived on to survive two world wars and die in relative obscurity in London in 1950.

A century of male dancers owe their creative inspiration to this indefinable man who made such an impact early in the 20th century and whose private life is one of the most talked about in dance history. What we would have given to see him perform, to be mesmerised by his magic in any one of his roles: the bestial slave of *Scheherazade*, the quivering animal of *Faune*, the pathetic puppet of *Petrushka*, the cunning Harlequin of *Carnaval* or the mystical spirit of *Spectre*. Like Shakespeare's man, Nijinsky had played many parts during those action-packed ten years: the performer who transformed himself completely in each role; the silent, introspective butterfly who only displayed the full colour of his wings on stage; the radical creator searching for alternative forms of language and the humanitarian projecting attitudes of peace.

On a more superficial level, he was viewed as the hero of the Parisian and London glitterati, the exotic lover of Diaghilev and the husband of Hungarian aristocrat Romola de Pulszky. Both of them needed him to reflect their glory and are interwoven into his story. Although Nijinsky would have been both a phenomenon and an enigma in any age, it is unlikely that we would be talking about the introverted Russian/Polish dancer today if it were not for the Russian visionary who dreamed of the possibilities of marrying Eastern culture with that of the West and the Hungarian girl who also loved him and was bewitched by his magic.

Nijinsky was lesser known as the family man – the father of two daughters – or the fallen artist, an exile from his native land, trapped in his own inner world.

Nijinsky would have had a memorable career as an actor/dancer without unleashing the radical choreographic ideas pulsating behind his publicly masked face. Diaghilev was a visionary marketer, unsurpassed at creating and selling artistic concepts, who promoted Nijinsky over the ballerina and gave him the opportunity to explore his creative ideas – the licence to unleash them on the largely unprepared public. One can only speculate what it must have been like to experience *Sacre, Jeux* or *Faune* by comparing them to later-century groundbreaking works of the 1980s, such as William Forsythe's *In the Middle Somewhat Elevated,* which strips the stage bare apart from the two small cherries suspended from the ceiling that give the ballet its title, or Mats Ek's *Giselle,* which sets the traditional Romantic classic in a contemporary lunatic asylum.

Like so many artists cut off in their prime, Nijinsky's fame intensified after his death. Yet his ballets died in the repertoire: a modified version of *Faune* was performed in Ballets Russes by the great dancers who followed him, Massine and Lifar; *Jeux* was dropped after its first season; Massine rechoreographed a relatively successful production of *Sacre* and *Till* was never seen in Europe and totally overlooked, although Romola Nijinsky did attempt to have it staged by the Paris Opera with Baryshnikov in the title role. In any age – let alone the self-conscious age of the 21st century,

Nijinsky has to be applauded for his single-minded commitment to creating choreography that was unfashionable – loathed by artists and audiences alike. Like all contemporary choreographers, his vision was way ahead of the audience's expectations. It is only in hindsight that he has been judged as a genius – the initiator of neoclassicism in dance and the instigator of the 20th-century school of modern dance.

It is only since contemporary critics took another look at his works through the diligent reconstructions of Ann Hutchinson Guest, Millicent Hodson and Kenneth Archer that Nijinsky was acknowledged as a choreographer of importance. Nijinsky was oblivious to the need to convince others of his ideas. He just developed them and they kept coming, even when he was diagnosed as not of right mind. The tragedy is that, for whatever reason, his mind became too clouded to transmit them to others. One cannot help wondering what kind of choreography he may have devised in the future. In history, these things happen, but what is it about this man that so intrigues the world, that it is still attempting to discuss?

It could well be his vision for mankind that he expressed through his art form and later in his drawings – which have been compared to those of Wassily Kandinsky, one of the pioneers of abstraction in western art – and his freewheeling kaleidoscope of written thoughts. On reading his diary again after absorbing others' opinions, his voice spoke with resounding clarity through his often manic rhymes and passionate rhythms. His clear views of universal values and respect for truth and beauty exhibit a sanity that we all could covet. It is a requiem, a soliloquy, a compassionate gospel: "Everything I write is a teaching essential to mankind .... I am the artist who loves all shapes and all kinds of beauty. Beauty is not a relative thing. Beauty is god. God is beauty with feeling."

Nijinsky was the lone crusader, outside of society. Frustrated with his inability to verbally communicate his thoughts and denied a means of physical expression, he resorted to clarifying his views on paper:

> *I am a man with a soul and therefore I weep when I am not understood .... I am not afraid of bullets and poison. I*

> *am afraid of spiritual death. I will not go insane, but I will weep and weep .... I am a man with love and men with love are simple .... I want love for people .... I want peace for all. I want love on earth.*

His poems are like song lyrics addressed to Romola, Frenkel and many others: "I want to tell you ...that I sleep I sleep I sleep .... I want to tell you that I am asleep but I am not asleep."

His legacy has lived on in the ballet world and through his fascinating family. One could assume that Nijinsky himself would have approved that its focus shifted to America, where he had been mostly happy and to which he had responded on his first arrival and retained memories of after the muddling of his mind.

They continued Nijinsky's original ideas in their individual ways:

ROMOLA

Romola was an extraordinary superwoman, liberated beyond her time and dauntless in her drive to keep her husband's name alive. From the moment she first saw him on the Budapest stage, Romola was obsessed with Nijinsky. She battled to communicate his ballet beliefs and preserve his legacy and rights. During his period of darkness, she struggled to claim he was cured and, after his death, continued to restlessly roam the world searching for love while still committed to the Nijinsky legacy. She lectured around the world on ballet issues, staged *Faune* and wrote *The Last Years of Nijinsky,* published in 1952; she brought numerous court cases against unjust claimants to his works, even suing Stravinsky for the rights to *Sacre.* She made a mission of trying to produce a film based on her *Nijinsky* biography, which became an ongoing saga lasting over twenty years. In 1940, she established Nijinsky Productions, Incorporated in New York and had high hopes of producing other films about ballet under the label of Ballet Miniatures. It was a tragedy that Nijinsky's performances and choreography were never filmed during his career or satisfactorily recreated. He was fascinated by the medium and had discussed it with Diaghilev. Romola's film project appeared to be jinxed: she relentlessly pursued the idea, using every possible connection. When the first contract foundered, she approached Alexander Korda in Hollywood and entered an agreement with him, which was several times postponed and eventually failed. In 1950, she offered exclusive rights to Alexander Paal of Alexander Films in Hollywood, who told her Gene Kelly wanted to be involved. Many of the lawsuits Romola brought over the next few years were over the rights to the film.

Romola envisioned making the film in Russia in a co-production with the Bolshoi and Kirov Ballets, with English-speaking actors. In 1960, she visited Russia for the first time to negotiate and inspect the original locations. It was a sad trip, as she had been convinced that Nijinsky would have improved if he had been able to return to his native land. However, she was feted as the widow of a national hero and Khrushchev presented her with a sable coat in memory of Fanny Elssler, who had received a full-length sable coat from Tsar Nicholas I as she was boarding the flight home.

Romola tried to make films on ballet for television; she wrote to actor John Gielgud for advice on the film and received a reply suggesting Yul Brunner as Nijinsky, with either Charles Laughton or Orson Welles in the role of Diaghilev. His ballet director niece Maina Gielgud took lessons from Nijinsky's co-star Karsavina. She says: "Nijinsky has always fascinated and almost haunted me. One gleans that he had a fascinating personality on stage – an extraordinary animal movement quality and of course the famous jump."

In 1962, Romola was planning to make a film of Nijinsky's last ballet *Till Eulenspiegel* and. in 1966. reached the tenth anniversary of the biographical film lawsuit. Tamara Nijinsky reports in her book that Rudolf Nureyev was suggested many times for the film "but allegedly demanded half a million dollars. Romola responded to the producers, in that case, she wanted one million dollars .... Romola stressed that as much as she admired Nureyev, he was not at all like her husband." Nevertheless, plans were announced in 1970 for Nureyev to take the part of Nijinsky in a film written by Edward Albee and directed by Tony Richardson. Discussions took place for a possible Broadway show as a forerunner to the film. Later, Romola suggested that Luchino Visconti direct the film and begged that Paul Schofield be offered the role of Diaghilev: She insisted that Nijinsky should be danced by the twenty-two-year-old Mikhail Baryshnikov, the "greatest living dancer and actor". However, the project was curtailed by Baryshnikov's lack of availability.

A later venture was the prospective filming of *Faune* and *Jeux* by Japanese dancer Hideo Fukagawa, to be rehearsed by Bronislava in 1972, which was thwarted by her death. It was the same year as the premiere of Maurice Bejart's ballet *Nijinsky, Clown of God.* The legend of Nijinsky is also believed to have inspired the classic ballet film *The Red Shoes.*

The saga of the Nijinsky film appeared endless and was, sadly, only realised after Romola's death. *Nijinsky* was the dream-child of choreographer/dancer Herbert Ross, with Alan Bates as Diaghilev and American Ballet Theatre soloist George de la Peña in the title role. Actress Lesley Brown played Romola and the film was well-supported balletically, with Carla Fracci as Tamara Karsavina and the *corps de ballet* of the London Festival Ballet (now English National Ballet).

Although it augured well with such an illustrious cast and great intent, the film was neither an artistic nor commercial success, a venture that Nijinsky's family would rather forget. They believed Paul Cox's abstract 2001 film, based on Nijinsky's diary, truly conveyed the spirit of the man and his art.

In 1976, the Paris Opera staged *Faune* in three versions – choreographed by Nijinsky, Maurice Bejart and Jerome Robbins.

Romola had aspired to immigrate to America with her husband and, during her latter years, maintained a residence in San Francisco. After her death from cancer in 1978, much of the focus of the Nijinsky legacy shifted to America. The original red notebooks in which Nijinsky poured his jumbled thoughts and had achieved notoriety as *The Diary of Vaslav Nijinsky* were acquired by the Dance Collection of the New York Public Library, which holds most of the documentation of his career.

Nijinsky collector John Neumeier still dwells on holding the precious notebooks in his hand when they were sold for the second time in the early 1990s: "Holding, touching, studying, feeling, turning page after page and then not buying." In the catalogue of the Dansmuseet exhibition to mark the fiftieth anniversary of Nijinsky's death, Neumeier writes:

> *I continue to collect, to search for new images – for more pictures to this puzzle – Nijinsky. I collect not to exhibit as a museum would do, but simply to live with these manifestations of a man I've learned truly to love – more and more deeply over the years.*

Much of the material for the exhibition came from his personal Nijinsky memorabilia, which has collecting since the age of ten. Neumeier choreographed the ballet *Nijinsky* for his Hamburg Ballet and presents a Nijinsky Festival with the company each year.

BALANCHINE

Diaghilev's last choreographer, Balanchine, became a major influence on dance, establishing it strongly within the American culture, extending its vocabulary and pushing its barriers in a wide body of work.

BRONISLAVA

Bronislava Nijinsky settled in California and collaborated with her daughter Irina (to whom she had passed on the family elongated Achilles tendon) in writing her memoirs. Irina remembers her mother responding to questions about books published about her brother – *Nijinsky* by Romola Nijinsky and *The Tragedy of Nijinsky* by Anatole Bourman: "The books are filled with half-truths and outright fantasies, not only about my brother, but also about my mother and father." She began planning her own book, *Early Memoirs,* based on her diaries, notebooks and letters and had completed the Russian manuscript when she died in 1971.

KYRA

The Nijinsky legacy was inherited by Kyra, who was living in San Francisco. She had been disconnected from the family at an early age but lived out her life in the shadow of her famous father. In many ways, her life echoed his; she was multiskilled in the creative arts – a talented performer, poet and painter. Both Nijinsky daughters had independently moved to the West Coast of the United States of America but continued to live separate lives until the death of their mother. By that time, Kyra was living in reduced circumstances, lonely, impoverished and struggling with her own unstable psyche – estranged from her son Vaslav Markevitch and his two children in Switzerland. She was deeply religious, and her wish to be buried in the order of St Francis Lazarus was honoured by her sister, Tamara, with whom she reunited shortly before her death.

TAMARA

The baton was passed to the second daughter Tamara, who had immigrated first to Canada and later to Phoenix, Arizona. Tamara describes herself as "a cocktail – my father was Russian Polish, my mother Hungarian, I was born in Austria, French was my first language (when they were living in Paris), but now I am American".

By a sad quirk of fate, Tamara grew up less aware of her father's fame than her actress grandmother's public profile in her native Hungary. She had a couple of early memories but had seen little of him during her childhood in Paris and the years in Hungary with her grandparents studying at drama school and her subsequent marriage.

Tamara finally came to know her father through her concentrated work on his journals.

It was due to her determination to restore Nijinsky's diary to its original form that the unexpurgated edition was published in French in 1995 and English in 1999.

By the time Tamara inherited responsibility for the Nijinsky legacy of fame and memorabilia, the Nijinsky Foundation started by Romola in London had fizzled out. Tamara rekindled the foundation in America and, with the assistance of her daughter Kinga, became committed to the mission to "preserve, promote the memory, art and legacy of Vaslav Nijinsky as a dancer and innovative choreographer and support research in performing arts medicine".

On my visit, I discovered her whole house to be a shrine to her father. Vaslav Nijinsky's world was recreated in Phoenix, Arizona. Tamara's house was peopled with Nijinsky's personal mementoes. Vaslav Nijinsky's paintings and drawings sit beside Ballet Russes posters, china and other memorabilia, a sculpture of the great Nijinsky, a comprehensive collection of books and writing. Irrespective of the material held in the Dance Collection of the New York Public Library, it is a Nijinsky worshipper's heaven.

Custody complications with Kinga's actor father prevented Tamara and her second husband, musician Laszlo (Laci) Weninger, from emigrating from the stringent socialist regime in Hungary after the Second World War. They lived through the uprising of 1956 and finally left Hungary for Montreal, Canada, in 1957, where they spent several years before moving to Arizona for Laszlo in 1961 to take up a position as a church organist in Phoenix – which, at the time, they had to look up on the map.

Tamara continued her career as a puppeteer in America, creating her own special platform for paying homage to her father with her traditional Indonesian wayang puppets – two *Le Spectre de la rose* puppets representing the characters created in Fokine's famous ballet by her father and her namesake, Tamara Karsavina. The puppets occupied pride of place in Tamara's Arizona home. Having worked as a puppeteer, teacher and librarian, Tamara led an active life in Phoenix supporting her church and the Hungarian community of the city and maintaining the Nijinsky legacy, travelling the world lecturing and promoting. Her tireless work has been recognised by the governments of France and Poland, which have both knighted her. She was awarded Chevalier de l'Ordre des Artes et des Lettres 1995; the Polish Order of Arts and Letters in 1997; and Officer de l'Ordre des Artes et des Lettres and La Grande Medaille (Vermeil) de la Ville de Paris in 2000. Tamara died in Arizona on 30 November 2017 at the age of 97.

KINGA

Just as Tamara's house is sacred to Nijinsky, her daughter Kinga Nijinsky Gaspers's home is a memorial to his wife, Romola. Her front door is painted the same shade of brilliant red favoured by her grandmother and she has inherited her exquisite oriental furniture, clothes and make-up, all of which found their place in the play *Madame Nijinsky* performed by Kinga in Phoenix and Budapest (where the story of Nijinsky and Romola began) for the Nijinsky anniversary in the year 2000.

Kinga's dinner guests sit at Romola's table and eat off her china using her cutlery. Kinga is a self-confessed frustrated dancer who, like both her parents and her illustrious grandmother Emilia Markus, turned to acting instead. Like her mother growing up in Hungary in the shadow of her famous grandmother and artistic lineage of the de Pulskys, Kinga grew up with an awareness of both her grandmother and matinee idol actor father Miklos.

This writer then witnessed Romola's granddaughter wearing Romola's red silk pyjamas, smoking her brand of cigarettes and wearing her own Helena Rubenstein shade of lipstick, publicly recreating the fascinating Romola's thoughts. In the eyes of the world, Romola too has remained an enigma, castigated by the homosexual world as the cause of Nijinsky's madness for "forcing him to marry her" and coming from a far worldlier viewpoint of life. To many people, she was perceived as grasping and scheming. It is an equation that Kinga has seen fit to set right. She believes Romola to have been unfairly judged. Kinga is an untiring upholder of the Nijinsky legacy, like her mother, and is also the recipient of awards from the French Government. She is an accomplished actress, musician and writer with an impeccable lineage in the arts: she started studying acting in Hungary with her father and wrote a thesis on her illustrious great-grandmother Emilia Markus for her Master of Arts in Theatre. Her son Mark and three grandchildren continue the illustrious lineage.

VASLAV MARKEVITCH

My visit to Vaslav in his home in Tuscany in the summer of 2005 has a huge bearing on this story. A dark-haired, strong-charactered, articulate man in his late sixties, Nijinsky's grandson and namesake has little contact with his relatives, whom he claims to have no rights to the artistic and spiritual Nijinsky legacy. His father Igor Markevitch remarried an Italian, and he is half-brother to musician/conductor Oleg Caetani.

Vaslav was very much at home in Italy, where he had recently returned at the time of my visit. He was known there as Marco Vinci. He is truly cosmopolitan – Russian/Polish parents, brought up by a family in Florence and sent to school in England. A consummate cultured European, multilingual and intellectual, Vaslav lived in Geneva for many years, where he worked for the International Red Cross. He has been married twice and has children and two grandchildren.

My visit teetered on near-disaster. He considered it his mission to correct the story of Nijinsky and outline the path to a better world. He claims to have inherited Nijinsky's insights along with some of his children and is working on assimilating information about global issues such as climate change. If he were alive today, his grandson believes, Nijinsky would not be a dancer, but possibly investigating space. Vaslav Markevitch died in Geneva in January 2024.

I am enriched by the knowledge of Nijinsky, Diaghilev, their world and the pre-revolution Russian ballet. Who was Nijinsky? When I embarked on the search for his story, Tamara Nijinsky told me to ask him for guidance. I visited the Imperial School in St Petersburg where he slipped on the floorboards and visualised him climbing the steep stone, well-worn steps. I followed in his footsteps up Rossi Street, Nevsky Prospect, beside the Fontanka Canal with its bronze horses and backstage at the Mariinsky Theatre.

I stood in front of his grave in the Montmartre Cemetery gazing at the memorial sculpture donated by Lifar and willed him to again to speak to me. He probably preferred to stay at rest. We can draw a fairly coherent picture of his genius as an artist – although I still cannot begin to imagine the impact of seeing him dance. Picture him moving towards us – his exotic Slavic face, mysterious eyes, animal grace, lithe body and current of electricity apace – but no, he remains elusive; a forerunner of a different race? A phenomenon still to analyse and emulate.

His career lasted a mere ten years, yet Nijinsky was one of the most influential figures in 20th-century dance. His legacy has enriched generations, yet so much remains unknown. Most people know of his legendary leap, but Nijinsky's genius has affected the art form in a multitude of ways, much of which I had been unaware: as a supreme dancer, interpretative role creator, visionary choreographer, humanitarian and spiritual guru. He was so much in advance of his time that he appeared more than mortal: his extraordinary story has endowed him with mythical status; his thoughts on mankind are only gradually being grasped. Much of the mystery surrounding Nijinsky stems from a lack of exact information: there is no film (maybe because Diaghilev had a horror of photographs), no moving record of his dancing or choreography, although there is, thankfully, a treasure trove of still photographs that capture the power of his interpretative dance.

But it is further fuelled by the mystery of the man himself – the varying perceptions of his psyche and his own perceptions of the world. Was this artist who came and went in such a blinding flash of brilliance a genius or a madman? Nijinsky had an intuitive understanding of his art. He lived his roles on stage. Such an artist occurs perhaps once a century.

Yet, offstage, people often spoke to him as if he were a child, as if his mind was slow. Like his fellow geniuses, Van Gogh and Schumann, he straddled the bridge between brilliance and insanity. His story can therefore be interpreted either way. It is his aura of mystery and unanswered questions, his lack of language offstage and mesmerising power onstage, that have continued to fascinate Nijinsky's followers and inspire them to probe the drama of his life and thoughts.

The memoirs of those surrounding Nijinsky during his life are priceless cameos of the time but vary in fact as well as perception.

We want to see him move; we want to understand him. We are still trying to fit together the pieces of the man. A gentle man, an altruistic being, a lover of mankind, a self-admitted "Man of Love, "a simple man, intelligent, humble, individual … striving to convey his code of ethics and belief in the connecting circles of dance and life." His image continues to inspire and intrigue – a genius ahead of his time The consequences of his thoughts remain in our consciousness and on our stages; his messages make more sense every day. Nijinsky's spirit lives on in every artist who strives for perfection and every choreographer who defies barriers to their art form, particularly dance.

ACKNOWLEDGEMENTS

This book began 20 years ago, when Alida Chase suggested the idea to the late Paul Cox, who was making a film about Nijinsky's diary. I would like to thank her, him, Paul's assistant Margot Wiburd, Aanya Whitehead and Kevin Lucas of Music Art Dance Films, for birthing this book by sending me to Phoenix to stay with Nijinsky's second daughter, Tamara.

In Phoenix, Tamara Nijinsky, her daughter Kinga Nijinsky Gaspers and her family welcomed me with warmth and generously offered me unlimited knowledge of their illustrious father and grandfather, Vaslav, and his wife Romola, which was enhanced by sleeping in a bedroom that served as a shrine to Nijinsky.

In New York, Susan and Paul Talbot generously offered me the hospitality of their beautiful brownstone home on the Upper East Side, from where I walked to the New York Public Library each day. The dedicated staff of the Jerome Robbins Dance Division were equally obliging in assisting me with my research. I came away with boxfuls of photocopies, in the mode of the era, that I have been enlightened by revisiting.

I am indebted to my dear friend, the late Sheila Drummond, for her literary advice and encouragement all along the way and to Christopher Lyndon-Gee for connecting me with Vaslav Markevitch in Italy.

More recently, Kyra Cox generously gave me access to her late father's drawing by Nijinsky given to him by the Nijinsky family, and Ellie Young arranged for David Tatnall to photograph it in the way it deserved.

My thanks to Kenneth Watkins, a long-time colleague at the Australian Ballet, David Hallberg for supporting the publication, Lyndell Pond and Renee Colquhoun for assisting with marketing and Donna Cusack for arranging for the Nijinsky ballet performance image. I am indebted to the long-time collector of Nijinsky memorabilia, John Neumeier, for granting me permission to quote his words and include the image.

Above all, I am forever grateful for the bond of the ballet family, the joy, ongoing support and the depth of experience offered by the dance world, introducing me to Nijinsky and all the other artists and arts workers who have enriched our lives and shown us a better world.

BIBLIOGRAPHY

Beaumont, Cyril, *Bookseller at the Ballet*: Cyril Beaumont, 1975

Benois, Alexandre, *Reminiscences of the Russian Ballet*: Translated by Mary Britnieva: Putnam, 1941

Buckle, Richard, *Diaghilev*: Athenaeum, 1979

Buckle, Richard, *Nijinsky*: Simon and Schuster, 1971

Buckle, Richard, editor, *Dancing for Diaghilev, the memoirs of Lydia Sokolova*: John Murray, London, 1960

Craft, Robert, Conversations with Igor Stravinsky: Penguin Books, 1958

Dolin, Anton, *Last Words*: Century Publishing, 1985

Drummond, John, *Speaking of Diaghilev*: Faber and Faber, 1997

Eksteins, Modris, *Rites of Spring*: Anchor Books, Doubleday, 1990

Figes, Orlando, *Natasha's Dance, A Cultural History of Russia:* Allen Lane The Penguin Press, 2002

Franks, A.H., *Twentieth Century Ballet*: Burke, London, 1954

Gadan, Francis and Maillard, Robert, *A Dictionary of Modern Ballet*: Translated from the French, Methuen, 1959

Garafola, Lynn, *Diaghilev's* Ballets Russes: Oxford University Press, 1989

Garcia – Marquez, Vincente, *Massine*: Nick Horne Books ((NHB), London, 1996

Gelati, Roland, *Nijinsky, The Film*: Paramount Pictures Corporation, 1980

Gold, Arthur and Fizdale, Robert, *The Life of Misia Sert*: Alfred A. Knopf, 1980

Grigoriev, S.L., *The Diaghilev Ballet 1909 – 1929,* Translated by Vera Bowen: Constable, 1953

Haskell, Arnold, *Balletomane at Large – An Autobiography*: Heinemann, London, 1972

Hill, Polly and Richard Keynes, editors, *Lydia and Maynard, the letters of Lydia Lopokova and John Maynard Keynes*: M Papermac (A Division of Pan Macmillan Publishers), London, 1992

Holyroyd, Michael, *Lytton Strachey*: Vintage (Random House), London, 1995

Jones, Colin, *Paris – Biography of a City:* Allen Lane, Penguin, 2004

Karsavina, Tamara, *Theatre Street*: Readers Union, Constable, 1950

Kirstein, Lincoln, *Nijinsky Dancing:* Alfred A.Knopf, 1975

Kochno, Boris, *Diaghilev and the Ballets Russes,* Translated from the French by Adrienne

Foulke: Allen Lane The Penguin Press, 1971

Krasovkaya, Vera, *Nijinsky,* Translated from the Russian by John E. Bowlt: Dance Horizons, Schirmer Books, 1979

Lieven, Prince Peter, *The Birth of the* Ballets Russes: Dover Publications, 1973

Lifar, Serge, translated by James Holman Mason, *Ma Vie – an autobiography*: Hutchinson of London

Lifar, Serge, translated by Gerard Hopkins, *The Three Graces – the Legends and the Truth*: Cassell, London, 1959

Magriel, Paul, Three Lives: Nijinsky, Palova and Duncan

Markevitch, Igor, *Made in Italy*: The Harvill Press, 1949

Naslund, Erik, *Nijinsky,* Dansmuseet exhibition catalogue, 2000

Nijinska, Bronislava, *Early Memoirs*: Holt, Rinehart and Winston, 1981

Nijinsky, Romola, *Nijinsky*: Sphere Books, 1933

Nijinsky, Romola, *The Diary of Vaslav Nijinsky*, 1936

Nijinsky, Romola, *The Last Years of Nijinsky*: Simon and Schuster, 1952

Nijinsky, Tamara, *Nijinsky and Romola*: Bachman& Turner, United Arts, 1991

Nijinsky, Vaslav, *The Diary of Vaslav Nijinsky* Unexpurgated Version, translated from the Russian by Kyril Fitzlyon, edited by Joan Accocella: Farrar, Straus and Giroux, 1995

Ostwald, Peter, *Nijinsky, A Leap into Madness*: A Lyle Stuart Book, published by Carol Publishing Group, 1991

Parker, Derek, *Nijinsky: God of the Dance*: Equation, 1988

Romanovsky-Krassinsky, HSH The Princess, *Dancing in Petersburg – the Memoirs of Kschessinska*, Translated by Arnold Haskell, published by Garden City, 1961

Roslavleva, Natalia, *Era of the Russian Ballet 1770-1965*, Victor Gollanz, 1966

Schneider, Ilya Ilyitch, *Isadora Duncan, the Russian Years*: Translated by David Magarshack: Macdonald & Co, 1968

Shead, Richard, *Ballets Russes*: Quarto Publishing, 1989

Sitwell, Osbert, *Left Hand Right Hand*: Macmillan & Co, 1949

Smakov, Gennady, *The Great Russian Dancers*: Alfred A. Knopf, 1984

MAGAZINES, PERIODICALS, LETTERS

Accocella, Joan, *The Lost Nijinsky*: The New Yorker, May 7, 2001

The Astruc (Gabriel) Papers: Dance Collection, Library and Museum of Performing Arts, New York Public Library

Ballet and Opera, September 1949

Crafoot, Leonard, *Nijinsky Speaks*: Play clippings, 1998

Colbert, Mary, A dream comes true as 'real' Nijinsky takes centre stage: The Sunday Age (in Toronto)

Letters to Diaghilev: The Dance Collection, New York Public Library

Four letters to Serge Diaghilev concerning Vaslav Nijinsky, January, 1929

Telegrams 1912-1914, Diaghilev: Dance Collection, Library and Museum of Performing Arts, New York Public Library

Diaghilev, Serge, *Around the World with the Russian Ballet*: Dance magazine, September 1979

Dornberg, John, A 700-year-old mine in Poland is a shrine to human ingenuity: Smithsonian, March 1994

Garafola, Lynn, *Aftermath of a Faun*: Dance magazine, December 1991

Gesmer, Daniel, *Still Grasping for Nijinsky's Elusive Legacy*: New York Times, August 27 2000

Gesmer, Daniel, *Revisioning Vaslav*: Ballet Review, Spring 2000

Guest, Ann Hutchinson, *Letter to the Editor*: Ballet Review, Spring 1995

Goldschmidt, Hubert, Ballet Review,*Millicent Hodson and Kenneth Archer*: *Till Eugenspiegel in Paris*: Ballet Review, Spring 1995

Harris, Dale, *Elusive Genius*: Ballet News, March 1981

Kisselgoff, Anna, *Who's Who in 'Nijinsky*:' New York Times, March 16, 1980

Kisselgoff, Anna, *Tracing the Echoes of Mallarme's Enigmatic Faun*: New York Times, April 9 1989

Kisselgoff, Anna, *Nijinsky Returns, with a Scarf and a Triple Kiss*: New York Times, March 5 2002

Neumeir, John, *Vaslaw clippings*: Dance Collection, Library and Museum of Performing Arts, New York

Nijinsky, Waslow, 1890 –1950, *Miscellaneous manuscripts*: Dance Collection, Library and Museum of Performing Arts, New York

Percival, John, London Festival Ballet at the Kennedy Center: Nureyev in Nijinsky's roles: Dance and Dancers, January 1979

Percival, John, *Ballet and its Heritage*: Ballet Review, Summer 1995

Philp, Richard, *Nijinsky, Nureyev, "Gods" of Dance*: Dance magazine, February 1995

Smith, Sid, *It's the season for a new 'Rite of Spring*':Chicago Tribune, October 7,2001

Wiley, Roland John, *About Nijinsky's Dismissal*: The Dancing Times, December 1979

Unattributed internet biographies of Pablo Picasso and Stephene Mallarme

FILM, VIDEO AND AUDIO

Jerome Robbins Archive, Dance Collection, Library and Museum of Performing Arts, New York Public Library:
L'apres midi d'un faune
Le Sacre du Printemps
Interview with Maurice Bejart,1972
Interview with Igor Markevitch: 1972
Interview with Cyril Beaumont: 1974
The Russian Ballet
The Diaries of Vaslav Nijinsky (original in Russian on microfilm)

OTHER SOURCES:

Nijinsky, biographical feature film directed by Herbert Ross, 1980
The Diaries of Vaslav Nijinsky, documentary drama directed by Paul Cox, 2002
Nijinsky, Death of a Faun, video of play by David Pownall, 1991

Photo courtesy of The Australian Ballet.
Callum Linnane in John Neumeier's Nijinsky, 2016.
Photo Lynette Wills.

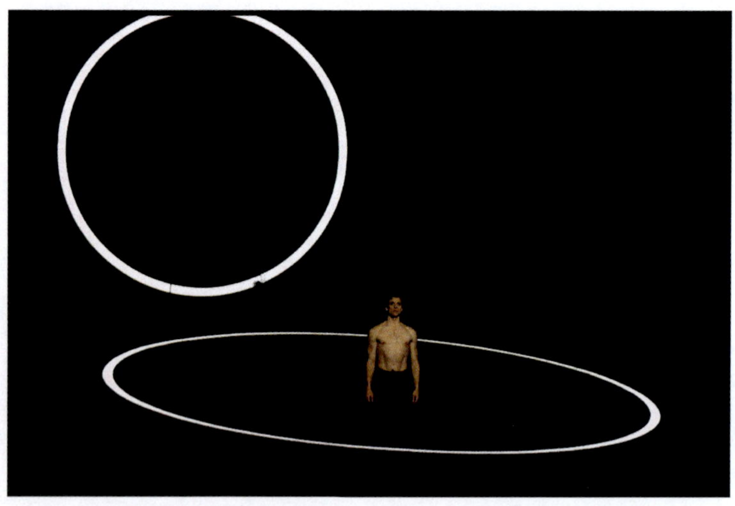

Photo courtesy of The Australian Ballet. Kevin Jackson in John Neumeier's Nijinsky, 2016. Photo Kate Longley